沙滩排球竞赛规则
2021—2024

中国排球协会　译定

人民体育出版社

图书在版编目（CIP）数据

沙滩排球竞赛规则.2021—2024/中国排球协会译
定. -- 北京：人民体育出版社，2023
ISBN 978-7-5009-6249-6

Ⅰ.①沙… Ⅱ.①中… Ⅲ.①沙滩排球运动—竞赛规
则—2021-2024 Ⅳ.① G842.4

中国版本图书馆 CIP 数据核字 (2022) 第 248965 号

*

人民体育出版社出版发行
北京中科印刷有限公司印刷
新　华　书　店　经　销

*

710×1000　16 开本　9.75 印张　150 千字
2023 年 3 月第 1 版　2023 年 3 月第 1 次印刷

*

ISBN 978-7-5009-6249-6

定价：48.00 元

社址：北京市东城区体育馆路 8 号（天坛公园东门）
电话：67151482（发行部）　　邮编：100061
传真：67151483　　　　　　　邮购：67118491
网址：www.psphpress.com

（购买本社图书，如遇有缺损页可与邮购部联系）

前　言

《沙滩排球竞赛规则 2021—2024》（以下简称"本规则"）是中国排球协会根据 2021 年国际排球联合会（简称"国际排联"，英文为 FIVB）第 37 次代表大会通过的英文规则《OFFICIAL BEACH VOLLEYBALL RULES 2021—2024》，组织有关人员翻译、审定的。

本规则适用于全国各级正式沙滩排球比赛。各地可在本规则的基础上，结合我国开展沙滩排球运动的实际情况，根据不同年龄层次、不同参与人群的需求，参考本规则灵活制定符合当地实际的规则，因地制宜地开展各类沙滩排球赛事，如三人制或四人制沙滩排球比赛，场地大小可适当调整，少儿比赛可降低球网高度等。其主要目的就是减小比赛难度、降低技术要求、增加比赛趣味性，以吸引更多人积极参与沙滩排球运动。

为帮助读者对规则进行深入的研究和学习，本规则后面附有英文版全文，以供读者对照参考。

在此，对在本规则翻译修改过程中给予大力支持的中国排球协会沙滩排球裁判委员会及沈阳体育学院表示感谢。本规则翻译过程中难免存在不足，欢迎批评指正。

欲了解我国沙滩排球运动发展的最新动态或与我们交流，请访问中国排球协会官方网站：www.volleychina.org。

中国排球协会
2022 年 4 月 6 日

目 录

比赛的特性 ·· 01

第一部分　规则与裁判工作的指导思想 ·· 03

第二部分　比赛规则 ··· 09

 第一章　比赛 ·· 11

  第一节　器材与设备 ·· 11

   1　比赛场地 ·· 11

    1.1　面积 ·· 11

    1.2　比赛场地的地面 ·· 11

    1.3　场地上的界线 ··· 12

    1.4　区与场地 ··· 12

    1.5　天气 ·· 12

    1.6　照明 ·· 12

   2　球网和网柱 ·· 13

    2.1　球网高度 ··· 13

    2.2　球网结构 ··· 13

    2.3　标志带 ·· 14

    2.4　标志杆 ·· 14

    2.5　网柱 ·· 14

    2.6　附属设备 ··· 14

   3　球 ··· 15

    3.1　标准 ·· 15

01

3.2　统一性 ·· 15
  3.3　4 球制 ·· 15

 第二节　比赛参加者 ·· 16

  4　比赛队 ·· 16
    4.1　队的组成 ·· 16
    4.2　队的位置 ·· 16
    4.3　装备 ·· 16
    4.4　服装的更换 ·· 17
    4.5　禁止的物品 ·· 17

  5　队的领导 ·· 17
    5.1　队长 ·· 18

 第三节　比赛方法 ·· 19

  6　得 1 分、胜 1 局与胜 1 场 ··· 19
    6.1　得 1 分 ·· 19
    6.2　胜 1 局 ·· 20
    6.3　胜 1 场 ·· 20
    6.4　弃权和阵容不完整 ··· 20

  7　比赛的组织 ··· 20
    7.1　挑边 ·· 20
    7.2　正式热身活动 ·· 21
    7.3　队的阵容 ··· 21
    7.4　队员的位置 ··· 21
    7.5　位置错误 ··· 21
    7.6　发球次序 ··· 22
    7.7　发球次序错误 ·· 22

 第四节　比赛行为 ·· 23

  8　比赛的状态 ··· 23
    8.1　进入比赛 ··· 23

8.2	比赛的中止	23
8.3	界内球	23
8.4	界外球	23

9　比赛中的击球 …… 24

9.1	球队的击球	24
9.2	击球的特性	25
9.3	击球时的犯规	26

10　球网附近的球 …… 26

10.1	球通过球网	26
10.2	球触球网	26
10.3	球入球网	27

11　球网附近的队员 …… 27

11.1	越过球网	27
11.2	进入对方空间、场区或无障碍区	27
11.3	触网	27
11.4	队员在球网附近的犯规	27

12　发球 …… 28

12.1	每局的第1次发球	28
12.2	发球次序	28
12.3	发球的允许	28
12.4	发球的执行	29
12.5	发球掩护	29
12.6	发球时的犯规	29

13　进攻性击球 …… 30

13.1	进攻性击球的特性	30
13.2	进攻性击球的犯规	30

14　拦网 …… 31

14.1	拦网	31
14.2	拦网触球	31
14.3	进入对方空间拦网	31

	14.4	拦网与球队的击球 ································· 31
	14.5	拦发球 ·· 32
	14.6	拦网犯规 ·· 32

第五节　间断、延误和局间休息 ·································· 33

15　间断 ··· 33
　　15.1　合法比赛间断的次数 ································· 33
　　15.2　合法比赛间断的次序 ································· 33
　　15.3　请求合法比赛间断 ···································· 33
　　15.4　暂停与技术暂停 ······································· 33
　　15.5　不符合规定的请求 ···································· 34

16　比赛的延误 ·· 34
　　16.1　延误的类型 ··· 34
　　16.2　延误的处罚 ··· 34

17　比赛的意外间断 ···································· 35
　　17.1　受伤或生病 ··· 35
　　17.2　外界干扰 ·· 36
　　17.3　被拖延的间断 ·· 36

18　局间休息与交换场区 ······························ 36
　　18.1　局间休息 ·· 36
　　18.2　交换场区 ·· 36

第六节　参赛者的行为 ··· 37

19　行为要求 ·· 37
　　19.1　体育道德行为 ·· 37
　　19.2　公正竞赛 ·· 37

20　不良行为及其判罚 ································· 37
　　20.1　轻微的不良行为 ······································· 37
　　20.2　给予判罚的不良行为 ································ 38
　　20.3　判罚的等级 ··· 38

20.4　局前和局间的不良行为 ··· 39

20.5　不良行为的种类及红黄牌的使用 ································ 39

第二章　裁判员及其职责与法定手势 ································ 40

第七节　裁判员 ··· 40

21　裁判团队和工作程序 ·· 40

21.1　组成 ·· 40

21.2　工作程序 ··· 40

22　第 1 裁判员 ·· 41

22.1　位置 ·· 41

22.2　权力 ·· 42

22.3　职责 ·· 42

23　第 2 裁判员 ·· 43

23.1　位置 ·· 43

23.2　权力 ·· 43

23.3　职责 ·· 44

24　挑战裁判员 ·· 45

24.1　位置 ·· 45

24.2　职责 ·· 45

25　替补裁判员 ·· 45

25.1　位置 ·· 45

25.2　职责 ·· 46

26　记录员 ·· 46

26.1　位置 ·· 46

26.2　职责 ·· 46

27　辅助记录员 ·· 47

27.1　位置 ·· 47

27.2　职责 ·· 47

28　司线员 ·· 48

28.1　位置 ·· 48

28.2 职责 ·· 48
29 法定手势 ·· 49
29.1 裁判员手势 ·· 49
29.2 司线员旗示 ·· 49

第三章　图表 ·· 50

图1：比赛场地 ·· 50
图2：比赛场区 ·· 51
图3：球网 ·· 52
图4a：球越过球网垂直平面进入对方比赛场区 ···························· 53
图4b：球越过球网垂直平面进入对方无障碍区 ··························· 54
图5：发球掩护 ·· 55
图6：完成拦网 ·· 55
图7：警告和判罚 ·· 56
　　7a：不良行为警告和处罚等级表及后续结果 ························ 56
　　7b：延误的处罚等级表及后续结果 ···································· 56
图8：裁判团队及其辅助人员的位置 ·· 57
图9：裁判员法定手势 ·· 58
图10：司线员法定旗示 ·· 65

第三部分　定义 ·· 67

附：本规则英文部分 ·· 72

比赛的特性

沙滩排球是一项两队运动员在由球网分开的沙地上进行比赛的运动。

每队可击球 3 次（包括拦网触球）将球击回对方场区。

在沙滩排球比赛中，一支球队胜 1 球可以得 1 分（每球得分制）。接发球队胜 1 球时得 1 分，同时获得发球权。每次换发球时发球队员必须轮换。

第一部分

规则与裁判工作的指导思想

介 绍

无论从哪个角度来看，沙滩排球都是世界上最成功、最受欢迎的运动之一，与其他运动相比，它的收视率更高，社交媒体上的关注者更多，注册运动员和业余球员的数量更多（且不断增加）。它动感、纯净、丰富多彩，尤其在各级别竞技比赛中，它呈现出的视觉和听觉盛宴能够满足每个人的需求。

简而言之，它**速度快、富有激情**而且充满**爆发力**。沙滩排球包含若干重要的重合要素，这些要素**相互作用**，使它成为一种独特的隔网球类运动，从而创造出一种区别于其他运动形式的特殊魅力。

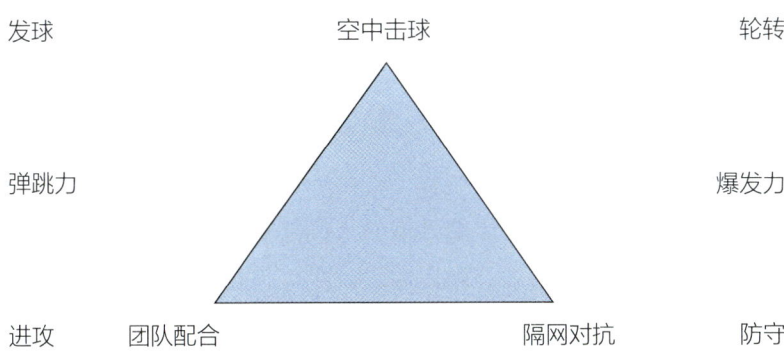

国际排联沙滩排球比赛是一项竞技性运动

沙滩排球运动起源于加利福尼亚海滩，竞赛潜力无限，展示出了其独特的文化、精神、创造力和美感。规则也应随之展现出这些品质。近年来，国际排联对沙滩排球项目进行了很大的调整，以满足现代观众的需要。

就这点而言，沙滩排球保持了它原有的特点和元素，使它仍然具有同其他隔网对抗类项目一样的特征：→发球→轮转（轮换发球）→进攻→防守→队员可以出现在场上任何位置。

沙滩排球运动发展到今天，更有爆发力，更具体验感。它具有快速和自由流畅的特点，也有运动员在观众众多的赛场上做出惊人之举。此外，沙滩排球与其他隔网对抗类项目相比，独特之处在于追求让球一直在空中飞翔——让球飞起来，每队在将球回击到对方之前可以在本方进行传球以创造机会，从而创造平等的得分机会。近年来，国际排联在技术使用方面进行了大量投资，利用视频挑战系统为运动员的努力提供公正性保障。国际排联鼓励促进流畅比赛的理念以满足观众娱乐的需求。比赛双方要利用规则这个平台，充分展示技术、战术和实力；也让运动员尽情发挥，以吸引更多现场和电视机前的观众，并营造出一个无与伦比的运动场面。

沙滩排球运动将会呈现出越来越美好的前景。

规则条文

本条文适用于广大沙滩排球运动参与者——运动员、教练员、裁判员、观众、解说评论员及其他人员。由于对规则的正确理解，教练员可以更加合理地组织队伍和部署战术，运动员可以更加淋漓尽致地发挥技战术水平。此外，对书面规则和实际行为内在联系的了解，可以使裁判员更加合理地做出公正的判罚。

沙滩排球运动具有娱乐性和竞争性。娱乐性可以激发人们参与的热情，并增进"乐趣"，形成健康的生活方式。竞争性使人们能够展示出最佳的能力、创造力、表达自由和拼搏精神。规则的设计就是为了让所有这些得以实现。

此介绍首先是把沙滩排球作为竞技体育项目来关注，而不是明确一名成功的裁判员所必需具备的素质。

在本规则框架内的裁判员应具备的素质

优秀裁判员的精髓是在比赛中保持执法的公平公正：

裁判员站在比赛场区的中间位置是平衡的象征，鼓励运动员们信任裁判员的行为。然而，裁判员必须是辅助者，而不是控制者；是乐队指挥，而不是独裁者；是有效的促进者，而不是"高效"的惩罚者。

通过了解制定规则的原因，明确制定规则的目的，裁判员就会成为整个比赛成功的一个重要组成部分，虽然很多时候他保持在后台的位置，只在必要时进行干预。可以说，一名优秀的裁判员通过执行规则，给所有参与者带来丰富的体验和享受。

对于阅读本规则的读者们，在遵循规则推动运动项目发展的同时，也要认真思考上述观点，这将有益于你更好地融入该项运动。

一起来吧！

让球飞起来！

读懂比赛！

第二部分

比赛规则

第一章　比赛

第一节　器材与设备

参照规则

1	比赛场地	

比赛场地包括比赛场区和无障碍区。它应是长方形且对称的。　　　　　　　　　　　　　　　　　　　1.1，图1

1.1	面积

1.1.1　比赛场区为长 16 米、宽 8 米的长方形，四周至少有宽 3 米的无障碍区。　　　　　　　　　　　　　　　　　图 2

比赛场地上方的无障碍空间从场地表面量起至少高 7 米，无障碍空间内不得有任何障碍物。

1.1.2　**国际排联比赛、世界性比赛和正式比赛中，无障碍区距离端线或边线至少 5 米，至多 6 米。无障碍空间应从场地表面量起至少高 12.5 米。**

1.2	比赛场地的地面

1.2.1　场地的地面必须由平整的沙子组成，尽可能平坦、划一，没有石块、壳状物及其他任何可能造成运动员割伤或受伤的杂物。

1.2.2　**国际排联比赛、世界性比赛和正式比赛中，沙地必须至少深 40 厘米，并由松软的细沙组成。**

1.2.3　比赛场地的地面不得有任何可能伤害运动员的隐患。

1.2.4　**国际排联比赛、世界性比赛和正式比赛中，场地用沙应被筛选至可接受的尺寸，不可太粗糙，不得有石块和危险的颗粒。沙子也不能太细，以免造成粉尘或使粉尘粘在皮肤上。**

1.2.5　**国际排联比赛、世界性比赛和正式比赛中，建议在中央场地覆盖防水布以应对下雨天气。**

1.3　场地上的界线

图 2

1.3.1　所有的界线宽均为 5 厘米。其颜色必须与沙地的颜色对比明显。

1.3.2　界线

两条边线和两条端线划定比赛场区的范围。没有中线。边线和端线都包括在比赛场区的面积之内。

场区的界线应由抗腐蚀材料的带子制成，露在地面的固定装置必须是柔软、有韧性的。

1.4　区与场地

比赛场地包含比赛场区、发球区和围绕在比赛场区周围的无障碍区。

1.4.1　发球区是端线后延伸至无障碍区边缘的宽 8 米的区域。

1.5　天气

天气绝不能给运动员带来任何受伤的危险。

1.6　照明

国际排联比赛、世界性比赛和正式比赛如在夜间举行，比赛场地的光照强度应在距比赛场表面高 1 米处达到 1000 至 1500 勒克斯。

2 球网和网柱

图3

2.1 球网高度

2.1.1 球网垂直设立在场地中央,球网的高度为男子 2.43 米、女子 2.24 米。

注:球网的高度可根据特定年龄组而有所区别,如下所示:

年龄组	女子	男子
16 岁及以下	2.24 米	2.24 米
14 岁及以下	2.12 米	2.12 米
12 岁及以下	2.00 米	2.00 米

2.1.2 球网的高度应用量高尺在比赛场区中间丈量。球网的高度(包括两条边线的上方)必须完全相同,并且不得超过官方规定高度 2 厘米。

2.2 球网结构

球网被拉紧时长 8.5 米、宽 1 米(±3 厘米),垂直置于比赛场区的中轴线上。

图3

球网由 10 厘米见方的网格编织而成。球网上下沿的全长各缝有宽 7~10 厘米的双层帆布带,最好为深蓝色或鲜明的颜色。球网上沿帆布带的两端各留有一个小孔,用绳索穿过小孔系在网柱上保持球网顶端被拉紧。

用一根柔软有韧性的钢丝贯穿上沿的帆布带,用一根绳索贯穿下沿的帆布带,使球网与网柱固定并保持球网顶部和底部被拉紧。允许在水平帆布带上设置广告。

国际排联比赛、世界性比赛和正式比赛中,在不影响运动员和官方工作人员视线的情况下,可以使用长 8 米的球网。该球网网格更小,球网末端至网柱之间可展示商

标。根据国际排联的规定，允许在上述材料上印制广告。

2.3 标志带

标志带是两条宽 5 厘米（与场地界线同宽）、长 1 米的有色带子，被分别垂直固定在球网上，并垂直于每条边线。标志带被视为球网的一部分。

14.1.1，图 3

标志带上允许设置广告。

2.4 标志杆

标志杆是一根有韧性的杆子，长 1.80 米、直径 10 毫米，由玻璃纤维或类似材料制成。

每根标志杆被固定在每条标志带的外沿。两根标志杆位于球网的不同侧面。

每根标志杆顶部高出球网 80 厘米，高出的部分每 10 厘米应涂有对比明显的颜色，最好为红白相间。

标志杆被视为球网的一部分，并被视为过网区的边界。

2.5 网柱

图 2，图 3

2.5.1
支撑球网的网柱位于每条边线外 0.7~1 米处。网柱的高度为 2.55 米，最好可调节。

国际排联比赛、世界性比赛和正式比赛中，网柱固定在两条边线外 1 米处。

2.5.2
网柱是光滑的圆柱，禁止通过拉线固定在地面上。其装置必须是没有危险且不存在障碍物的。网柱必须用保护垫包裹起来。

2.6 附属设备

所有附属设备都必须符合国际排联标准。

第二部分 比赛规则

3 球

3.1 标准

球应是圆形的,由不吸水的柔软材料(皮革、人造皮革或类似材料)制成,以更适合室外条件,即使下雨时也能进行比赛。球的内部为橡胶或类似材质制成的可充气球胆。合成皮革材料的批准应由国际排联的章程确定。

颜色:单一的浅色或彩色。

圆周:66 至 68 厘米。

重量:260 至 280 克。

气压:0.175 至 0.225 千克/平方厘米(171 至 221 毫巴或百帕)。

3.2

3.2 统一性

在一场比赛中所有的用球,其周长、重量、气压、型号、颜色等都必须是统一标准的。

国际排联比赛、世界性比赛和正式比赛必须使用经国际排联批准的球,除非国际排联另有说明。

3.1, 23.2.8

3.3 4 球制

国际排联比赛、世界性比赛和正式比赛应使用 4 球制。 在这种情况下,设 6 名捡球员:无障碍区的 4 个角落各 1 名,第 1、2 裁判员后面各 1 名。

图 8

第二节　比赛参加者

参照规则

4　比赛队

4.1　队的组成

4.1.1　一支球队只能由 2 名队员组成。

4.1.2　只有记录在记录表上的两名队员才有权参加比赛。

4.1.3　其中一名队员应作为队长并在记录表上注明。

4.1.4　**国际排联比赛、世界性比赛和正式比赛中，运动员在比赛中不得接受外部的帮助或指导（例外情况：参照各年龄段比赛的具体规程以及洲际比赛第 1 和第 2 阶段的具体规程）。**

4.2　队的位置

球队席（包括每边 2 张座椅）必须距边线 5 米，距记录台不少于 3 米。

4.3　装备

队员的装备包括短裤或泳装。除比赛规程有特殊规定外，队员可选择穿比赛服或运动背心。运动员可戴帽子或头巾。

4.1.1

4.3.1　**国际排联比赛、世界性比赛和正式比赛中，根据比赛规程，同队队员服装颜色和款式必须一致，服装必须干净。**

4.3.2　除第 1 裁判员特许外，队员必须赤脚比赛。

4.3.3　队员的比赛服（如经允许可以不穿上衣时，则为短裤）必须分别标有号码 1、2。

4.3.3.1　号码必须标在胸前（或短裤前面）。

4.3.3.2　号码必须与比赛服颜色明显不同且至少高 10 厘米。号码笔画的宽度至少为 1.5 厘米。

4.4　服装的更换

如一场比赛中双方球队到达场地后穿着同样颜色的比赛服，应挑边决定由哪队更换服装。

第 1 裁判员可以允许一名或多名队员：

4.4.1　穿袜或鞋比赛；

4.4.2　在局间可更换潮湿的比赛服，前提是新换的服装也须符合比赛规程和国际排联的规定；

4.4.3　若队员提出请求，则第 1 裁判员可以允许其穿内衣和训练裤进行比赛。

4.3.3

4.5　禁止的物品

4.5.1　队员禁止佩戴可能对其造成伤害或使其人为获利的物品。

4.5.2　队员可以戴眼镜或隐形眼镜，但风险自负。

4.5.3　队员允许使用起到保护或支撑作用的加压护具（带衬垫的伤病保护装置）。

国际排联比赛、世界性比赛和正式比赛中的成年组比赛，这些护具或紧身衣作为比赛服装的一部分，颜色必须相同。

也可以使用黑色、白色或中性色，但同队两名队员穿戴的颜色必须一致。

5　队的领导

队长对该队的行为和纪律负责。

5.1 队长

5.1.1 比赛开始前，队长：

a）在记录表上签字；

b）代表本队进行挑边。

5.1.2 比赛中，只有队长有权在死球时，就下列 3 种情况与裁判员交流：   8.2

5.1.2.1 请求对规则和规则的执行进行解释。如果队长对解释不满意，应立即告知第 1 裁判员启动抗议程序的意愿。

5.1.2.2 请求允许：

a）更换服装或装备；

b）核对发球队员号码；

c）检查球网、球、场地等；

d）整理场地界线。

5.1.2.3 请求暂停   15.2.1,15.4.1

注：队员必须得到裁判员的批准才能离开比赛场地。

5.1.3 比赛结束时：

5.1.3.1 双方队员感谢裁判员和对方队员，队长在记录表上签字确认比赛结果；

5.1.3.2 队长如果曾向第 1 裁判员提出过启动抗议程序，并且未能当场解决，则有权通过正式的书面抗议程序进行确认，并于赛后填写在记录表上。   5.1.2.1

第三节　比赛方法

参照规则

6　得1分、胜1局与胜1场

6.1　得1分

6.1.1　得分

一支球队得1分：

6.1.1.1　成功地使球落在对方场区地面上； 图9（14）

6.1.1.2　当对方出现犯规时；

6.1.1.3　当对方受到判罚时。

6.1.2　犯规

一支球队的比赛行为违反了比赛规则（或以其他方式违反规则），即为"犯规"。裁判员根据规则进行判断和处理。

6.1.2.1　如果两个或更多的犯规连续发生，则只判第1个。

6.1.2.2　如果双方队员同时出现犯规，则判"双方犯规"，该回合重新进行。 图9（23）

6.1.3　回合和完整的回合

回合是从发球队员击球瞬间开始，直至成为死球的比赛行为过程。一个**完整的回合**是可赢得1分的比赛行为过程。这包括： 8.1, 8.2, 12.2.2.1, 12.4.4, 22.3.2.2

——判罚得分。

——未在规定时间内将球发出并导致失去发球权。

6.1.3.1 如果发球队赢得一个回合，则得 1 分并继续发球。

6.1.3.2 如果接发球队赢得一个回合，则得 1 分并获得发球权。

6.2	胜 1 局	
	每局（决胜局除外）由先得 21 分并至少超过对方 2 分的球队获胜。当比分为 20-20 时，比赛将继续进行至某队领先 2 分（22-20、23-21，以此类推）时为止。	图 9（9）

6.3	胜 1 场	
6.3.1	一场比赛由赢得两局胜利的球队获胜。	图 9（9）
6.3.2	当局分为 1-1 时，决定胜负的第 3 局要进行至 15 分并至少领先对方 2 分。	

6.4	弃权和阵容不完整	
6.4.1	如果一支球队被召唤后拒绝参赛，则宣布该队为弃权。这场比赛以 0-2 的局分和 0-21、0-21 的比分计为失利。	
6.4.2	未准时到达比赛场区的球队被宣布为弃权。	6.4.1
6.4.3	被宣布一局或一场比赛"阵容不完整"的球队输掉这一局或这一场比赛。应判对方获得该局或该场比赛胜利的必要分数和局数。阵容不完整的队保留其已得分数和局数。	6.2, 6.3, 7.3.1

国际排联比赛、世界性比赛和正式比赛中，采用小组赛单循环赛制时，上述规则 6.4 将根据国际排联公布的具体比赛规程而调整，对弃权和阵容不完整的情况进行处理。

7	比赛的组织

7.1	挑边

第 1 裁判员应在正式热身活动之前主持挑边，确认第 1

局先发球的球队和比赛场区。

7.1.1　挑边应在双方队长都在场的情况下进行。

7.1.2　挑边获胜方可在以下两种情况中选择其一：

7.1.2.1　发球权或接发球；

或

7.1.2.2　比赛场区的某一边。

挑边失利方从余下一项中选择。

7.1.2.3　第 2 局开始前，第 1 局挑边失利方可以在 7.1.2.1 或 7.1.2.2 中选择。

决胜局前重新进行挑边。

7.2　正式热身活动

在比赛开始前，如另有场地供比赛队进行热身活动，则每队在网前有 3 分钟的正式热身时间；否则每队可在网前正式热身 5 分钟。

7.3　队的阵容

7.3.1　每队的两名队员必须自始至终参加比赛。　　　　4.1.1

7.4　队员的位置

当发球队员击球时，双方队员（发球队员除外）必须都在本方场区内。

7.4.1　队员在场内可随意站位。场上没有固定的位置。

7.5　位置错误

7.5.1　没有位置错误犯规。

7.6 发球次序

7.6.1　发球次序必须在整局比赛中保持一致（在队长挑边后立即确定）。

7.6.2　当接发球队获得发球权时，其发球队员轮转。

7.7 发球次序错误

7.7.1　没有按照发球次序发球为发球次序犯规。该队失 1 分且对方获得发球权。 　　图 9（13）

7.7.2　记录员必须正确指示发球次序，并在鸣哨发球前纠正任何有错误的发球队员。

第四节 比赛行为

参照规则

8 比赛的状态

8.1 进入比赛

经第1裁判员允许、从发球队员击球瞬间开始即为进入比赛。　　　12, 12.3

8.2 比赛的中止

当任一裁判员因比赛中出现犯规而鸣哨时,比赛从犯规一刻起中止;若无犯规,比赛则从裁判员鸣哨一刻起中止。

8.3 界内球

在任何时间,球的任何部位触及比赛场区的地面包括触及界线,都被视为界内球。　　　图 9(14), 图 10(1)

8.4 界外球

下列情况为界外球:

8.4.1	球完全落在界线以外的地面上(即没有接触到界线);	1.3.2, 图 9(15), 图 10(2)
8.4.2	球触及比赛场区外的物体或非比赛人员;	图 9(15), 图 10(4)
8.4.3	球触及标志杆、网绳、网柱或标志带外侧的球网部分;	2.3, 图 3, 图 4a, 图 9(15), 图 10(4)

8.4.4	在发球或第 3 次击球后，球的部分或整体从过网区外完全越过球网的垂直平面（规则 10.1.2 除外）。	2.3, 10.1.2, 图 4a, 图 9(15), 图 10(4)
8.4.5	球的整体从网下空间穿过。	图 4a, 图 9(22)

9 比赛中的击球

每队只能在本方比赛场区及空间内击球（规则 10.1.2 除外）。   10.1.2

但可以越出本方的无障碍区或越过记录台及其延伸空间救球。

9.1 球队的击球

比赛中队员与球的任何接触都被视为击球。

每队最多可击球三次将球从球网上空击回至对方场区。如果超过三次，则判为"四次击球"。

球队的击球行为不仅包括队员的主动击球，也包括其与球的无意接触。

9.1.1	连续击球	
	一名队员不得连续击球两次（规则 9.2.2.2, 9.2.2.3, 14.2 和 14.4.2 除外）。	9.2.2.1, 14.2,14.4.2, 图 9(17)
9.1.2	同时击球	
	两名队员可以同时触球。	
9.1.2.1	同队的两名队员同时触球时，计为两次击球（拦网除外）。	14.2

如果他们同时去击球但只有其中一名队员触到球，则只记为一次击球。

如果他们之间发生冲撞，不算犯规。

9.1.2.2 当双方队员在网上同时触球后，比赛仍在进行，获得球的一方可再击球三次。如果球落在某方场区外，判对方击球出界。

9.1.2.3 如果双方队员在网上同时触球造成球的短暂停留，比赛继续进行。　　9.1.2.2

9.1.2.4 如果双方队员在网上同时触球后球触及标志杆，则该回合重新进行。

9.1.3 借助击球

在比赛场地内，队员不得在比赛场地内借助同伴或任何物体的支持进行击球。

但是，一名队员可以挡住或拉住同队另一名即将犯规（触网或干扰对方比赛等）的队员。

9.2 击球的特性

9.2.1 球可以触及身体的任何部位。

9.2.2 球不能被接住或抛出。它可以向任何方向弹出。　　9.3.3

9.2.2.1 同时触球：　　9.2.1

球可以触及身体的不同部位，但必须是同时触及。

9.2.2.2 连续触球：　　9.3.4

球队第 1 次击球时，除上手传球动作外，允许在同一击球动作中连续触球。如果是使用上手传球，即使是同一击球动作，在击球过程中也不允许连续触球。

9.2.2.3 在拦网时，允许一名或更多的拦网队员在同一拦网动作中连续触球；　　14.2

9.2.2.4 在防守急难球时，球在手中允许有短暂停留，包括使用上手传球动作。

9.3 击球时的犯规

9.3.1	4 次击球：一支球队连续击球 4 次。	9.1, 图 9(18)
9.3.2	借助击球：队员在比赛场地借助同伴或任何物体的支持进行击球。	9.1.3
9.3.3	持球：球被接住或抛出；而不是被弹击出（规则 9.2.2.1、9.2.2.2 除外）。	9.2.2, 图 9(16)
9.3.4	连击：一名队员连续击球两次，或球连续触及其身体的不同部位。	9.1.1, 9.2.2.2, 图 9(17)

10 球网附近的球

10.1 球通过球网

10.1.1	球必须通过球网上空的过网区进入对方场区。过网区是球网垂直平面的一部分，其范围是：	图 4a
10.1.1.1	下至球网上沿；	
10.1.1.2	两侧至标志杆及其延伸空间；	
10.1.1.3	上至天花板或建筑物（如果有）。	
10.1.2	球的整体或部分从过网区以外的空间飞入对方无障碍区时，在下列情况下可在本队击球次数之内将球击回：	9.1, 图 4b
10.1.2.1	球的整体或部分必须从过网区外的同侧空间被击回。对方不得阻碍此次击球。	图 4b
10.1.3	球的整体通过球网以下垂直平面为"界外球"。	
10.1.4	队员可以进入对方场区将从过网区外越过球网的球或尚未完全通过球网以下垂直平面的球击回。	10.1.3

10.2 球触球网

	球越过球网时可以触及球网。	10.1.1

10.3 球入球网

10.3.1	球入球网后,在该队3次击球的范围内可以再次被击出。	9.1
10.3.2	如果球击破球网或使球网坠落,该回合取消并重新进行。	

11 球网附近的队员

11.1 越过球网

11.1.1	拦网时,允许拦网队员越过球网触球,但不得在对方进攻性击球前干扰对方。	14.1, 14.3
11.1.2	进攻性击球后,允许该队员的手越过球网,但击球时必须在本方场地空间。	

11.2 进入对方空间、场区或无障碍区

11.2.1	在不妨碍对方比赛的情况下,允许队员进入对方空间、场区或无障碍区。	10.1.4

11.3 触网

11.3.1	在击球动作中,队员触及标志杆之间的球网为犯规。击球动作包括但不限于起跳、击球(或试图击球)、落地并准备好下一动作。	11.4.3, 22.3.2.3.c 26.3.2.2, 图3
11.3.2	队员可以触及网柱、网绳或标志杆外侧的其他任何物体包括球网本身,但不得干扰比赛(规则9.1.3除外)。	
11.3.3	由于球被击入球网而造成的球网触及对方队员,不算犯规。	

11.4 队员在球网附近的犯规

11.4.1	对方队员进攻性击球前,在对方空间触及球或对方队员。	图9(20)
11.4.2	队员从网下穿越进入对方空间并干扰对方比赛。	

11.4.3　队员干扰比赛包括下列情况（不限于此）： 11.3.1, 图3

——击球时，触及标志杆或标志杆之间的球网；

——借助标志杆之间的球网支持身体平衡；

——通过触网使本方获利；

——试图妨碍对方合法的击球；

——拉拽球网。

队员在球附近试图击球，即使没有触球也被认为是击球动作。

队员触及标志杆外侧的球网不是犯规（规则9.1.3除外）。

12　发球

正确的发球队员在发球区内击球进入比赛的动作为发球。

12.1　每局的第1次发球

12.1.1　每局挑边时选择发球权的球队首先发球。 6.3.2, 7.1

12.2　发球次序

12.2.1　队员必须遵循记录表上记录的发球顺序。

12.2.2　在每一局的第1次发球后，发球的队员依如下顺序确定：

12.2.2.1　当发球队赢得一个回合时，原发球队员继续发球。

12.2.2.2　当接发球队赢得一个回合时，该队获得发球权，并由上次没有发球的队员发球。

12.3　发球的允许

第1裁判员检查双方队员已做好比赛准备，发球队员已站在发球区并持球在手时，鸣哨允许发球。 图9(1)

12.4 发球的执行

12.4.1 球被抛起或被持球手松开后,应用一只手或手臂的任何 图 9(10)
部分将球击出。

12.4.2 球只能被抛起或从手中松开一次,但在手中摆弄球是被
允许的。

12.4.3 发球队员可在发球区内任意移动。发球队员在击球时或 1.4.2,
跳发球起跳时,不得触及场区(包括端线)或发球区以 图 9(22),
外的地面,脚不得伸至端线下。 图 10(4)

击球后,发球队员可以踏及或落在发球区外或场区内。
由于发球队员触动沙子而造成的界线移动不算犯规。

12.4.4 发球队员必须在第 1 裁判员鸣哨允许发球后 5 秒钟内将 图 9(11)
球击出。

12.4.5 裁判员鸣哨允许发球前的发球无效,该球重发。 图 9(23)

12.4.6 在发球队员将球抛起或松开持球手之后,如果球落地时
没有被发球队员触碰或被接住,则被视为一次发球。

12.4.7 不允许试图进一步发球。

12.5 发球掩护 图 9(12)

12.5.1 发球方队员不得利用掩护阻挡对方观察发球队员的击球 图 5
动作和球的飞行路线。

12.5.2 在发球时,球飞到球网垂直平面之前,发球方队员利用挥 图 5
臂、跳跃或侧向移动来遮挡发球队员击球动作和球的飞行
路线,构成发球掩护。如果接发球队能够明显看见其中一
种情况(击球动作或飞行路线),则不构成发球掩护。

12.6 发球时的犯规

12.6.1 发球犯规

下列犯规被判为发球犯规,应交换发球权。发球队:

12.6.1.1	发球次序错误；		12.2, 图 9(13)
12.6.1.2	不符合发球的规定。		12.4

12.6.2 发球击球后的犯规

球被正确发出后，出现下列情况仍被判为发球犯规：

12.6.2.1	球触及发球方的队员或球的整体没有从过网区通过球网垂直平面；		图 9(19)
12.6.2.2	界外球；		8.4, 图 9(15)
12.6.2.3	球越过发球掩护的队员。		图 5

13 进攻性击球

13.1 进攻性击球的特性

13.1.1 除发球和拦网外，所有直接朝向对方的击球都是进攻性击球。

13.1.2 球的整体通过球网垂直平面或触及对方队员，则完成进攻性击球。

13.1.3 任何队员可以对任何高度的球完成进攻性击球，但触球时必须在本方场区空间（规则 13.2.4、13.2.5 除外）。　　13.2.4, 13.2.5

13.2 进攻性击球的犯规

13.2.1	在对方空间内击球。		13.1.2, 图9(20)
13.2.2	击球出界。		8.4，图 9(15)
13.2.3	完成进攻性击球时张开手指或手指没有完全并拢、用指尖触球。		图 9(21)
13.2.4	对整体高于球网上沿的对方发球完成进攻性击球。		图 9(21)
13.2.5	用上手传球完成进攻性击球时，传球轨迹没有垂直于双肩连线，但试图传给同伴的球除外。		图 9(21)

14 拦网

14.1 拦网

14.1.1 拦网是队员靠近球网、在高于球网处阻挡对方来球的动作，而不必考虑接触球时的高度。但触球时，身体必须有一部分高于球网上沿。

14.1.2 试图拦网

没有触及球的拦网动作为试图拦网。

14.1.3 完成拦网

当拦网队员触及球时视为其完成拦网。 图 6

14.1.4 集体拦网

两名队员彼此靠近进行拦网为集体拦网，其中一人触球则完成拦网。

14.2 拦网触球

在一个动作中，球可以连续（迅速而连贯）地触及一名或两名拦网队员。这仅算作该队的一次击球。拦网时身体的任何部位都可以触球。 9.1.1,9.2.3

14.3 进入对方空间拦网

拦网时，队员可以将手或手臂伸过球网，但不得干扰对方击球。在对方队员进攻性击球之前，过网拦网不得触球。 13.1.1

14.4 拦网与球队的击球

14.4.1 拦网触球算作球队的一次击球。拦网的球队在拦网触球后只能再击球两次。

14.4.2 拦网后的第 1 次击球可以由任何一名队员进行，包括拦网时已经触球的那名队员。

| 14.5 | 拦发球 | 图 9(12) |

禁止拦对方的发球。

| 14.6 | 拦网犯规 | |

14.6.1　在对方进攻性击球之前，拦网队员在对方场区的空间内 14.3, 图 9(20)
触球。

14.6.2　从标志杆外侧的对方空间内拦网。

14.6.3　队员拦对方发球。　　　　　　　　　　　　　　图 9(12)

14.6.4　拦网出界。　　　　　　　　　　　　　　　　　图 9(24)

第五节　间断、延误和局间休息

参照规则

15　间断

间断是从一个完整的回合之后至第 1 裁判员发出下一次发球的哨音之间的时间。

合法比赛间断只有暂停。

图 9(4)

15.1　合法比赛间断的次数

每局比赛中，每队最多可以请求一次暂停。

15.2　合法比赛间断的次序

15.2.1　在同一次比赛间断内，双方球队可依次请求暂停。

15.2.2　不能更换队员。

15.2.3　在请求被拒绝并被判罚延误后的同一次比赛间断内（即在下一个完整的回合结束前），不允许请求任何合法比赛间断。

15.3　请求合法比赛间断

只有队长可以请求合法比赛间断。

15.4　暂停与技术暂停

15.4.1　请求暂停必须在比赛中止后、裁判员鸣哨允许发球前，并使用相应的手势。暂停时间为 30 秒钟。

图 9(4)

15.4.2　国际排联比赛、世界性比赛和正式比赛中，在第 1 局和第 2 局，每当双方比分之和为 21 分时，有一次 30 秒钟的技术暂停。如果主办方提出申请且国际排联予以批准，暂停和技术暂停的时长可以进行调整。

15.4.3	决胜局（第 3 局）没有"技术暂停"；每支球队只可以请求一次 30 秒的暂停。	
15.4.4	在所有合法间断（包括技术暂停）和局间休息时，队员必须到指定的运动员席休息。	15.5,16.1

15.5 不符合规定的请求

下列情况为不符合规定的暂停请求：

15.5.1	正在一个回合中或者在裁判员鸣哨允许发球的同时或之后提出请求；	6.1,3
15.5.2	无请求权的队员提出请求；	
15.5.3	超过规定次数的请求；	15.1
15.5.4	同一支球队在同一场比赛中任何进一步的不当请求被视作延误。	图 9(25)

16 比赛的延误

16.1 延误的类型

一支球队拖延比赛继续进行的不正当行为为延误，包括但不限于：

16.1.1	在裁判员鸣哨恢复比赛后，拖延暂停时间；	
16.1.2	再次提出不符合规定的请求；	15.5
16.1.3	拖延比赛（正常情况下，从上一个回合结束到裁判员鸣哨发球之间的时间最多为 12 秒）；	
16.1.4	球队成员拖延比赛。	

16.2 延误的处罚

16.2.1	"延误警告"和"延误判罚"是对球队延误比赛的处罚。

16.2.1.1 延误比赛的处罚对全场比赛有效。

16.2.1.2 所有延误比赛的处罚都被记录在记录表上。

16.2.2 一名成员在比赛中的第 1 次延误将受到"延误警告"的处罚。 图 9(25)，图 7b

16.2.3 在同一场比赛中，同队的任何成员第 2 次以及其后任何类型的延误都构成犯规，并且都应给予"延误判罚"：失 1 分并由对方发球。 图 9(25)，图 7b

16.2.4 赛前和局间的延误处罚在下一局中进行。

17 比赛的意外间断

17.1 受伤或生病

17.1.1 如果比赛中出现严重事故，裁判员必须立即中断比赛，并允许医疗援助进入场区。

然后，该回合重新进行。

17.1.2 一名受伤或生病的队员最长可被给予 5 分钟的恢复时间。裁判员必须同意指定的医护人员进入比赛场区治疗受伤队员。只有第 1 裁判员能允许运动员离开比赛场地而不予判罚。当治疗结束或无法提供治疗时，比赛必须继续进行。第 1 裁判员鸣哨并要求运动员继续比赛。此时，只有受伤队员能决定自己是否适合继续比赛。

如果这名队员在恢复时间结束时不能恢复或不能回到比赛场地，则该队被宣布为阵容不完整。 6.4.3, 7.3.1

在极端的情况下，赛会的医生可以反对受伤队员继续比赛。

注：受伤恢复时间从经过官方认证的该赛事医务人员抵达比赛场区治疗受伤队员时开始。如果该赛事没有提供经过官方认证的医务人员，或者队员选择由自己的医务人员进行治疗，则恢复时间将从裁判员允许时开始。

17.2 外界干扰

如果比赛中出现任何外界干扰，比赛都应停止且该回合重新进行。

17.3 被拖延的间断

17.3.1 发生任何突发状况妨碍比赛时，第 1 裁判员、赛事组织者和管理委员会（如有）应决定采取相应措施以恢复正常的比赛状态。

17.3.2 如果一次或数次间断的发生时间累计不超过 4 小时，这场比赛都将在已有得分的基础上继续进行，不必顾及是在原比赛场区还是其他比赛场区进行。

17.3.3 如果一次或数次间断的发生时间累计超过 4 小时，全场比赛重新进行。

18 局间休息与交换场区

18.1 局间休息

18.1.1 两局之间的时间为局间休息。所有局间休息时间均为1分钟。

局间休息时，应进行交换场区（按要求）并在记录表上登记球队下局的发球次序。 图 9(3)

决胜局前的局间休息，裁判员根据规则 7.1 主持挑边。

18.2 交换场区

18.2.1 双方比分之和每积 7 分（第 1、2 局）或 5 分（第 3 局）时交换场区。 图 9(3)

18.2.2 交换场区时，双方球队必须立即进行，不得延误。

若未及时交换场区，则在发现错误时立即交换。

交换场区时比分保持不变。

02

第二部分　比赛规则

第六节　参赛者的行为

参照规则

19　行为要求

19.1　体育道德行为

19.1.1　参赛者必须了解并遵守沙滩排球比赛规则。

19.1.2　参赛者必须以良好的体育道德行为服从裁判员的裁定，不允许进行争辩。

　　　　如果有疑问，可以并只能通过队长提请解释。　　　　5.1.2.1

19.1.3　参赛者必须克制那些旨在影响裁判员判断或掩盖本队犯规的动作或态度。

19.2　公正竞赛

19.2.1　参赛者的行为必须符合"公正竞赛"的精神，不仅对裁判员，而且对其他工作人员、对手、同队队友以及观众都要尊重、有礼貌。

19.2.2　比赛中，同队队员之间的交流是被允许的。　　　　5.2.3.4

20　不良行为及其判罚

20.1　轻微的不良行为

　　　　轻微的不良行为不受处罚，但第 1 裁判员有责任防止运动员出现接近处罚级别的不良行为。　　　　5.1.2,21.3

　　　　分以下两个阶段进行：

　　　　阶段 1：通过队长给予口头警告。

　　　　阶段 2：给予一名球队成员黄牌警告。这一正式警告本　　　　图 9(5)

身不是处罚，而是标志着该队员（进而该队）已经达到了被处罚的程度。该警告登记在记录表上，但不会造成直接后果。

20.2 给予判罚的不良行为

一名球队成员对裁判员、对手、同队队友或观众的不良行为按其严重程度分为三类。　　　　　　　4.1.1

20.2.1　粗鲁行为：违背文明或道德原则的举止。

20.2.2　冒犯行为：诽谤、侮辱性的言语或手势，包括任何表示出蔑视的行为。

20.2.3　侵犯行为：人身攻击或带有侵略性的、威胁性的行为。

20.3 判罚的等级

第 1 裁判员根据不良行为的程度进行判断，分别给予以下处罚：判罚、判罚出场、取消比赛资格，并将其登记在记录表上。　　　　　　　　　　　　　　　图 7a

20.3.1 判罚

用于粗鲁行为或同一名队员在同一局中粗鲁行为的再犯。在前两次行为中，每次判罚该队失 1 分且由对方获得发球权。同一局中第 2 次粗鲁行为的队员将被判罚出场，该队员在随后每局的粗鲁行为也会受到处罚。　　图 9(6)

20.3.2 判罚出场

第 1 次出现冒犯行为即被判罚出场。该队员必须离开比赛场地，并且其所在球队该局比赛被宣布为阵容不完整。　　6.4.3, 7.3.1, 图 9(7)

20.3.3 取消比赛资格

第 1 次出现人身攻击行为或者带有威胁性的（或含蓄的）侵略行为都会被予以取消比赛资格的处罚。该队员必须　　6.4.3, 7.3.1,

离开比赛场地，并且其所在球队该场比赛被宣布为阵容不完整。 图 9(8)

不良行为的处罚见《不良行为处罚等级表》。 图 7a

20.4　局前和局间的不良行为

任何发生在局前或局间的不良行为都应按照《不良行为处罚等级表》进行处罚，并在下一局中执行。 图 7a

20.5　不良行为的种类及红黄牌的使用

图9（5、6、7、8）

警告：不处罚——阶段 1：口头警告； 20.1

　　　　　　　阶段 2：出示黄牌。

判罚：处罚——出示红牌。 20.3.1, 图 7a

判罚出场：处罚——单手持红黄牌。 20.3.2, 图 7a

取消比赛资格：处罚——双手分持红黄牌。 20.3.3, 图 7a

第二章　裁判员及其职责与法定手势

第七节　裁判员

参照规则

21　裁判团队和工作程序

21.1　组成

一场比赛的裁判团队由以下人员组成：

——第 1 裁判员；　　　　　　　　　　　　　　　　22

——第 2 裁判员；　　　　　　　　　　　　　　　　23

——挑战裁判员（可适用的比赛）；　　　　　　　　24

——替补裁判员（可适用的比赛）；　　　　　　　　25

——记录员；　　　　　　　　　　　　　　　　　　26

——4 名（或 2 名）司线员。　　　　　　　　　　　28

其位置如图 8 所示。

国际排联比赛、世界性比赛和正式比赛中，另设一名辅助记录员。　27

21.2　工作程序

21.2.1　比赛进行中只有第 1 裁判员和第 2 裁判员可以鸣哨：

21.2.1.1　第 1 裁判员鸣哨发球，该回合开始；　　　图 9（1）

21.2.1.2 第 1 裁判员和第 2 裁判员在确定已发生犯规并明确其性质的前提下，鸣哨表示该回合结束。

21.2.2 在球成死球时，裁判员可能会鸣哨以表示他们同意或拒绝一支球队的请求。

21.2.3 当裁判员鸣哨**中止**该回合比赛后，应立即以法定手势表明： 22.2.1.2, 29.1

21.2.3.1 如果第 1 裁判员鸣哨，应依次指出：

　　a）应发球的队； 图 9(2)

　　b）犯规的性质；

　　c）犯规的队员（必要时）。

21.2.3.2 如果第 2 裁判员鸣哨，应依次指出：

　　a）犯规的性质；

　　b）犯规的队员（必要时）；

　　c）跟随第 1 裁判员的手势指出应发球的队。 图 9(2)

　　这种情况下，第 1 裁判员不用指出**犯规性质和犯规队员**，只指出**应发球的队**。

21.2.3.3 在双方都犯规的情况下，第 1、2 裁判员都要依次指出： 图 9(23)

　　a）犯规的性质；

　　b）犯规的队员（必要时）；

　　之后，由第 1 裁判员指出接下来应发球的队。 图 9(2)

22　第 1 裁判员

22.1　位置

第 1 裁判员站在与记录员相对的球网一端的裁判台上执行其职责。他的视线水平位置应高出球网上沿约 50 厘米。 图 1，图 8

22.2 权力

22.2.1 第 1 裁判员自始至终领导该场比赛，对所有裁判团队的所有成员和球队成员行使权力。

在比赛中，第 1 裁判员的判定是最终判定。如果发现裁判团队其他成员的判定有误，他有权改判。

第 1 裁判员甚至可以撤换任何不能正确履行其职责的裁判团队成员。

22.2.2 掌控捡球员和平沙员的工作。

22.2.3 有权决定涉及比赛的一切事宜，包括规则中没有提及的问题。

22.2.4 队员不允许对其判定进行任何讨论。

但是，当队长提出请求时，第 1 裁判员应对其判定所依据的规则和规则的执行给予解释。

如果队长不同意该解释并正式提出抗议，第 1 裁判员应允许启动抗议程序。

22.2.5 在比赛前和比赛中，第 1 裁判员负责决定赛场条件是否符合比赛要求。

22.2.6 第 1 裁判员根据导致队员最终受伤或生病的具体情况，同意启动医疗援助并掌握恢复时间。 17.1.2

22.3 职责

22.3.1 比赛前，第 1 裁判员：

22.3.1.1 检查比赛场地、球和其他器材的状况；

22.3.1.2 主持双方队长挑边；

22.3.1.3 掌握双方球队的热身活动。

22.3.2 比赛中，第 1 裁判员有权：

22.3.2.1 向球队提出警告；

22.3.2.2 对不良行为和延误比赛的行为进行处罚。

22.3.2.3 判定：

  a）发球队员犯规和发球掩护犯规；   图 5

  b）击球时的犯规；

  c）高于球网的犯规和主要（但不限于）发生在进攻方一侧的队员错误触及球网的行为；

  d）球完整地从球网下方空间穿越；   图 9(22)

  e）发出的球和第 3 次击出的球越过第 1 裁判员一侧的标志杆上方或外侧。

22.3.3 比赛结束后，第 1 裁判员检查记录表并签字。

23　第 2 裁判员

23.1　位置

第 2 裁判员站在比赛场区外侧靠近网柱的地方，与第 1 裁判员相向而立执行自己的职责。   图 1, 图 8

23.2　权力

23.2.1 第 2 裁判员是第 1 裁判员的助手，但也拥有他自己的管辖范围。   23.3

当第 1 裁判员不能继续自己的工作时，第 2 裁判员可以代替其工作。

23.2.2 对于其权限以外的犯规可以出示手势，但不得鸣哨，也不得对第 1 裁判员坚持自己的判断。

23.2.3 掌控记录员的工作。

23.2.4 向第 1 裁判员报告任何不良行为。

23.2.5	有权允许暂停和交换场区并掌握其持续时间，拒绝不符合规定的请求。	图 9(3、4)
23.2.6	检查每支球队请求暂停的次数，并在该队暂停结束后告知第 1 裁判员和相关队员。	
23.2.7	在第 1 裁判员准许一名队员接受医疗援助的情况下，第 2 裁判员应在此过程中予以协助，包括掌握恢复时间。	17.1.2
23.2.8	在比赛中检查球是否仍符合规则的要求。	
23.2.9	如果第 1 裁判员不能在决胜局前主持挑边，则由第 2 裁判员执行。之后，第 2 裁判员必须将所有相关信息通知记录员。	

23.3　职责

23.3.1	每局比赛开始前以及任何必要的时候，第 2 裁判员掌握记录员工作并检查发球队员是否正确。	
23.3.2	比赛中，第 2 裁判员对下列情况做出判断、鸣哨并做出手势：	
23.3.2.1	网下穿越进入对方场区和空间干扰了对方；	11.2, 图 9(22)
23.3.2.2	主要（但不限于）发生在拦网方一侧的队员错误触及球网的行为以及队员错误触及第 2 裁判员一侧标志杆的行为；	11.3.1
23.3.2.3	球触及场外物体；	8.4.2, 8.4.3, 图 9(15), 图 10(4)
23.3.2.4	包括发球过程在内，球的整体或部分越过过网区以外的球网到达对方场区或触及第 2 裁判员一侧的标志杆；	8.4.3, 8.4.4, 图 3, 图 4a, 图 9(15)
23.3.2.5	当第 1 裁判员处于不易观察的位置时球与沙地的接触；	
23.3.2.6	球的整体在对方网下空间时被救回。	图 9(22)
23.3.2.7	发出的球和第 3 次击出的球越过第 2 裁判员一侧的标志	

02
第二部分 比赛规则

杆上方或外侧。

23.3.3 比赛结束后，第 2 裁判员检查记录表并签字。

24 挑战裁判员

国际排联比赛、世界性比赛和正式比赛如果使用视频挑战系统（VCS），则必须另设一名挑战裁判员。

24.1 位置

挑战裁判员在由国际排联技术代表指定的独立的挑战区内执行其职责。

24.2 职责

24.2.1 挑战裁判员管理挑战程序，并确保该程序按照现行挑战规则进行。

24.2.2 挑战裁判员在执行其职责的过程中应身着正式裁判服。

24.2.3 在挑战程序完成后，挑战裁判员向第 1 裁判员告知犯规的性质。 21.2.3.1，图 9(2)

24.2.4 比赛结束后，挑战裁判员在记录表上签字。

25 替补裁判员

国际排联比赛、世界性比赛和正式比赛中，所有含电视转播的比赛和使用视频挑战系统（VCS）的比赛，必须设一名替补裁判员。

25.1 位置

替补裁判员在独立的位置执行其职责，该位置依国际排联场地布局而定。

25.2 职责

替补裁判员有义务：

25.2.1	在执行其职责过程中身着正式裁判服。	
25.2.2	当第 2 裁判员缺席或不能继续工作时，或者第 2 裁判员成为第 1 裁判员后，替补裁判员替代第 2 裁判员工作。	23.2.1
25.2.3	协助第 2 裁判员管理无障碍区。	图 9
25.2.4	介绍运动员完毕后，立即将 4 个比赛球交给第 2 裁判员。	3.3
25.2.5	在第 2 裁判员核对完发球队员后，递给第 2 裁判员 1 个比赛用球。	22.2.2
25.2.6	协助第 1 裁判员指导平沙员的工作。	
25.2.7	在使用视频挑战系统的情况下，替补裁判员监督记录员在电子记录表上填写挑战程序全过程。	24

26 记录员

26.1 位置

记录员坐在第 1 裁判员对面的记录台处，面对第 1 裁判员执行其职责。 图 1，图 8

26.2 职责

记录员根据比赛规则，配合第 2 裁判员填写记录表。

记录员根据自己的职责，通过蜂鸣器或其他发声装置通知违规行为或者向裁判员发出信号。

26.2.1 在比赛前和每局前，记录员：

26.2.1.1 按照现行比赛程序登记本场比赛和参赛队的数据，并获取双方队长的签字；

26.2.1.2 记录每支球队的发球次序。

26.2.2　比赛中，记录员：

26.2.2.1 记录得分；

26.2.2.2 掌握各队发球次序，如有任何错误，应在发球击球前给予提示；

26.2.2.3 记录检查暂停的次数，并通知第 2 裁判员；

26.2.2.4 通知裁判员不符合规定的暂停请求； 15.5

26.2.2.5 交换场区和每局比赛结束时，通知裁判员；

26.2.2.6 记录各种处罚和不符合规定的请求；

26.2.2.7 在第 2 裁判员的指导下记录其他事件，如受伤恢复时间、被拖延的间断、外界干扰等；

26.2.2.8 掌握局间休息。

26.2.3　比赛结束后，记录员：

26.2.3.1 记录最终结果；

26.2.3.2 如果有提出抗议的情况并得到第 1 裁判员事先同意，记录或允许队长将有关抗议的内容写在记录表上； 5.1.2.1, 5.1.3.2

26.2.3.3 记录员在记录表上签字后，依次取得双方队长和裁判员们的签字。

27　辅助记录员

27.1　位置

图1, 图8

辅助记录员坐在记录员身旁的记录台处执行其职责。

27.2　职责

辅助记录员协助记录员进行管理工作。

如果记录员无法继续工作，则由辅助记录员替代记录员工作。

27.2.1 比赛前和每局前，辅助记录员：

27.2.1.1 检查记分牌显示的所有信息是否正确。

27.2.2 比赛中，辅助记录员：

27.2.2.1 用标有数字 1 或 2 的号码牌指出每支球队应发球队员的号码；

27.2.2.2 发现任何错误时立即用蜂鸣器通知裁判员；

27.2.2.3 操作记录台的手动翻分牌；

27.2.2.4 检查各记分牌是否正确显示；

27.2.2.5 掌握技术暂停开始和结束的时间；

27.2.2.6 必要时，填写好备用记录表并交给记录员。

27.2.3 比赛结束后，辅助记录员：

27.2.3.1 在记录表上签字。

28　司线员

28.1　位置

如果只使用 2 名司线员，则他们站在距离每名裁判员右手最近的场区角端，斜向位于场角 1 至 2 米。　图1, 图8

他们各自负责自己一侧的端线和边线。

国际排联比赛、世界性比赛和正式比赛中，如果使用 4 名司线员，他们应分别站在无障碍区内距每个场区角端 1 至 3 米处，即位于他们各自负责界线的假想延长线上。

28.2　职责

28.2.1 司线员通过使用司线旗（40 厘米 x40 厘米）来执行其　图10

职责：

28.2.1.1 每当球落在他们所负责的界线附近时，示以"界内"或"界外"（注：主要由离球的飞行线路最近的司线员负责出旗）； 8.3, 8.4 图 10(1,2)

28.2.1.2 触及接球队员身体后出界的球，示以"触手出界"； 8.4, 图 10(3)

28.2.1.3 球触及标志杆、发出的球以及球队第 3 次击球时，球从过网区外过网等； 8.4.3, 8.4.4, 10.1.1, 图 4a, 图 10(4)

28.2.1.4 在发球击球的瞬间，任何队员（发球队员除外）的脚踏及场区之外； 7.4, 12.4.3, 图 10(4)

28.2.1.5 发球队员脚的犯规； 12.4.3, 图10(4)

28.2.1.6 队员击球时触及其一侧的球网上沿 80 厘米标志杆或干扰比赛； 11.3.1, 11.4.4, 图 3, 图 10(4)

28.2.1.7 球从过网区外侧越过球网进入对方场区，或触及其所在一侧的标志杆； 10.1.1, 图 4a, 图 10(4)

28.2.1.8 比赛回合中拦网队员触及球。

28.2.2 当第 1 裁判员询问时，司线员必须重复旗示。

29 法定手势

29.1 裁判员手势

裁判员必须用法定手势指出鸣哨的原因（犯规性质或准许比赛中断的目的等）。手势应保持片刻，如果是单手做手势，应使用与犯规球队或提出请求球队同侧的手表示。 图 9

29.2 司线员旗示

司线员必须用法定旗示指出犯规的性质，旗示应保持片刻。 图 10

第三章 图表

图1：比赛场地

参见规则：1, 22.1, 23.1, 26.1, 27.1, 28.1

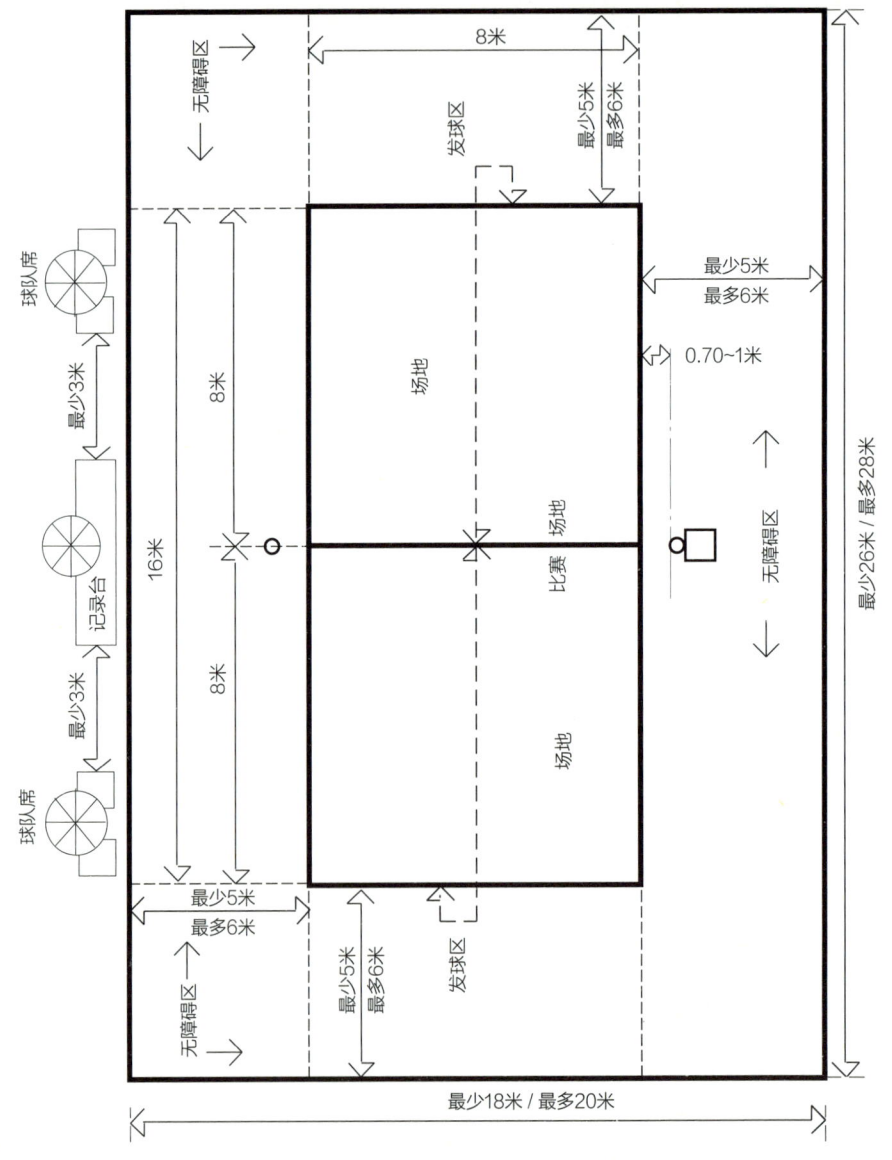

图 2：比赛场区

参见规则：1.1, 1.3, 2.5

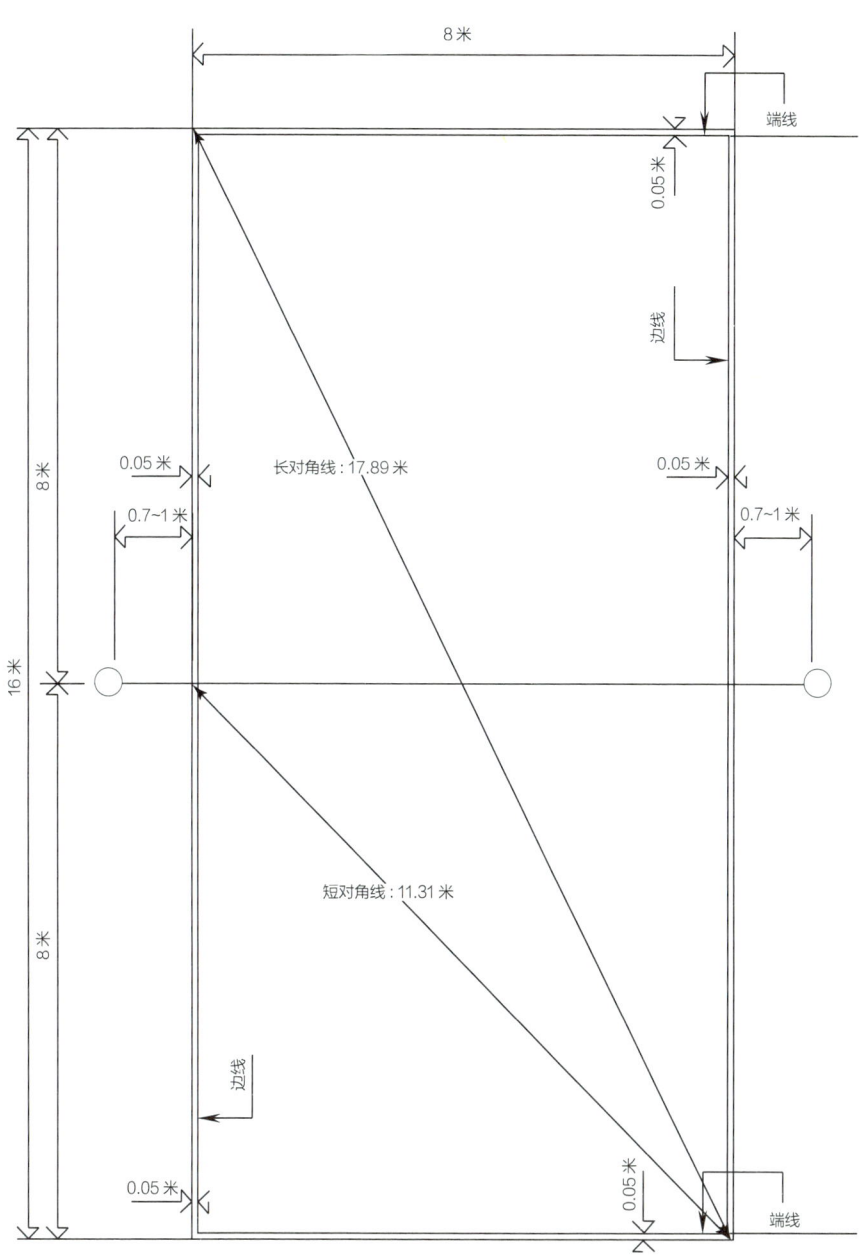

图3: 球　网

参见规则：2, 8.4.3

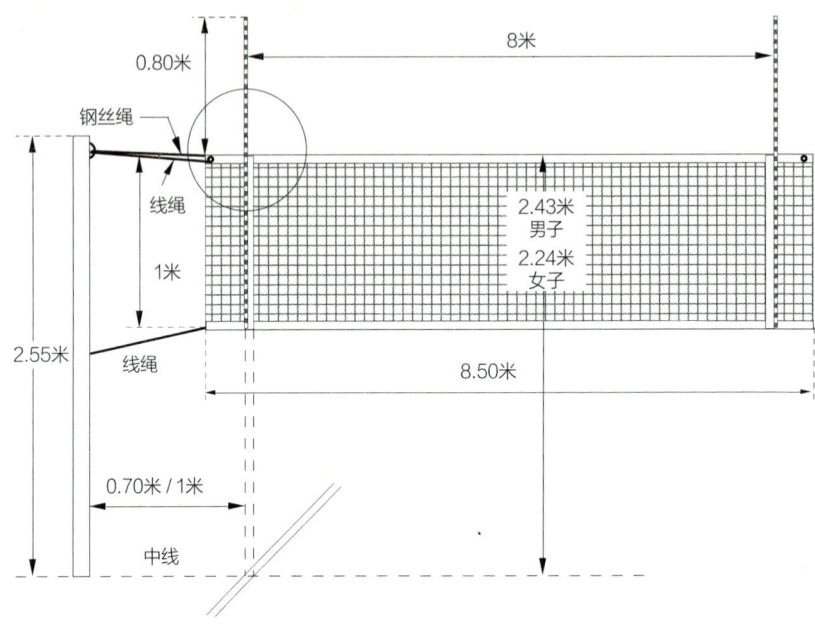

国际排联比赛、世界性比赛和正式比赛中，可根据规则2.1进行调整。

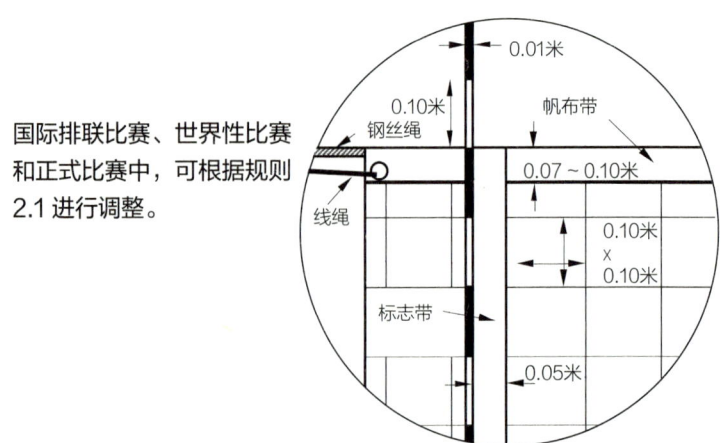

图 4a: 球越过球网垂直平面进入对方比赛场区

参见规则：8.4.3, 8.4.4, 8.4.5, 10.1.1, 23.3.2.4, 28.2.1.3, 28.2.1.7

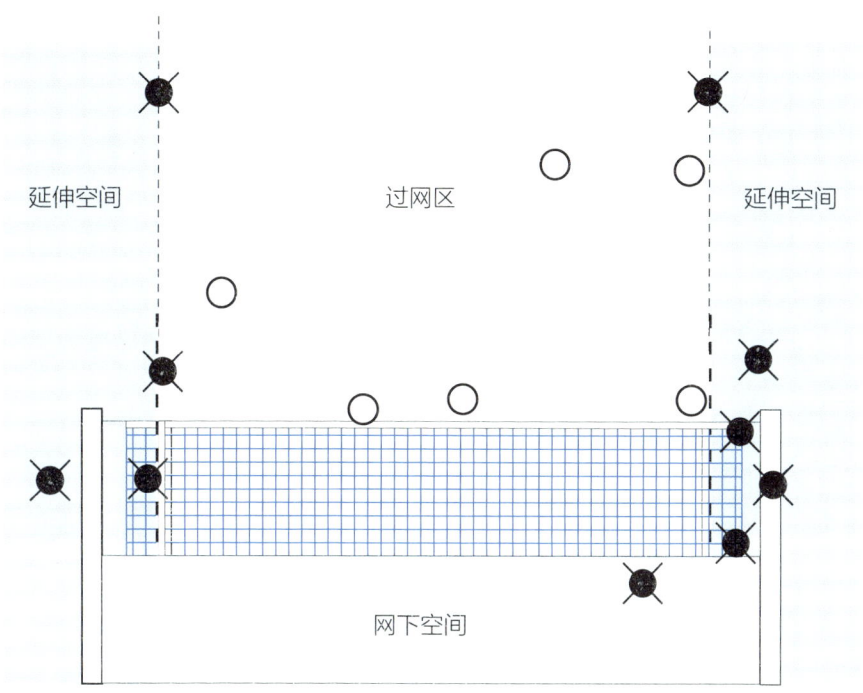

图 4b: 球越过球网垂直平面进入对方无障碍区

参见规则：10.1.2, 10.1.2.1

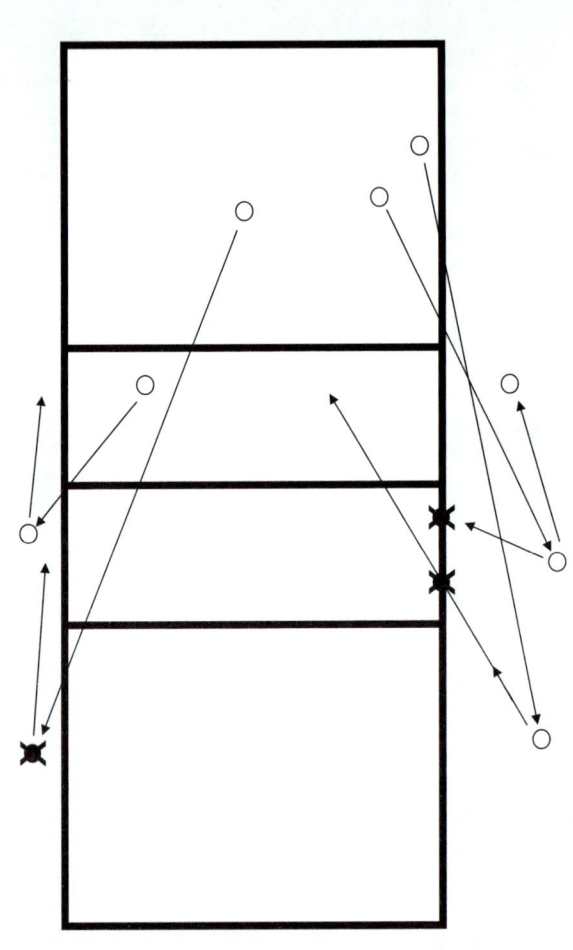

✖ = 犯规
O = 正确

图 5: 发球掩护

参见规则：12.5.1, 12.5.2, 12.6.2.3, 22.3.2.3

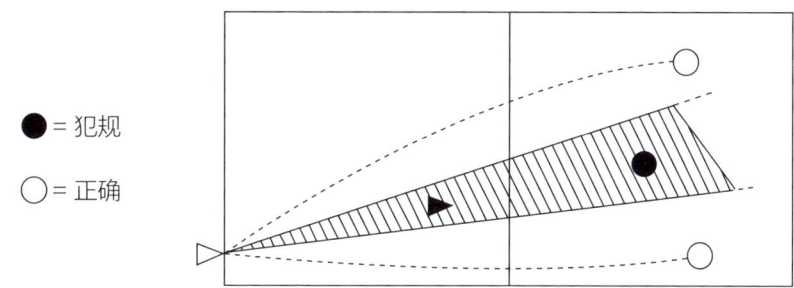

● = 犯规

○ = 正确

图 6: 完成拦网

参见规则：14.1.3

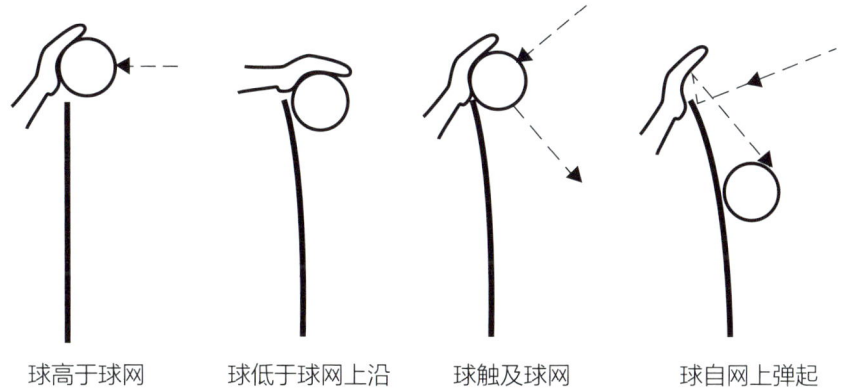

球高于球网　　球低于球网上沿　　球触及球网　　球自网上弹起

55

图7: 警告和判罚

7a: 不良行为警告和处罚等级表及后续结果

参见规则：20.3, 20.4, 20.5

类别	次数	犯规队员	判罚	出牌	结果
轻微不良行为	第1阶段	任一队员	不判罚	无	仅防止再犯
	第2阶段			黄牌	
	再次发生		被视为粗鲁行为	如下所示	如下所示
粗鲁行为（同一局）	第1次	任一队员	判罚	红牌	失一分对方发球
	第2次	此队员再犯	判罚	红牌	失一分对方发球
	第3次	此队员再犯	判罚出场	单手持红黄牌	队伍阵容不完整输掉这局比赛
粗鲁行为（下一局）	第1次	任一队员	判罚	红牌	失一分对方发球
冒犯行为	第1次	任一队员	判罚出场	单手持红黄牌	队伍阵容不完整输掉这局比赛
	第2次	此队员再犯	取消比赛资格	双手分持红黄牌	队伍阵容不完整输掉这场比赛
侵犯行为	第1次	任一队员	取消比赛资格	双手分持红黄牌	队伍阵容不完整输掉这场比赛

7b: 延误的处罚等级表及后续结果

参见规则：16.2.2, 16.2.3

类别	次数	犯规队员	警告或判罚	出牌	结果
延误	第1次	任何队员	延误警告	手势图25 出示黄牌	防止再犯不判罚
	第2次及其后	任何队员	延误判罚	手势图25 出示红牌	失一分对方发球

图 8: 裁判团队及其辅助人员的位置

参见规则：3.3, 21.1, 22.1, 23.1, 26.1, 27.1, 28.1

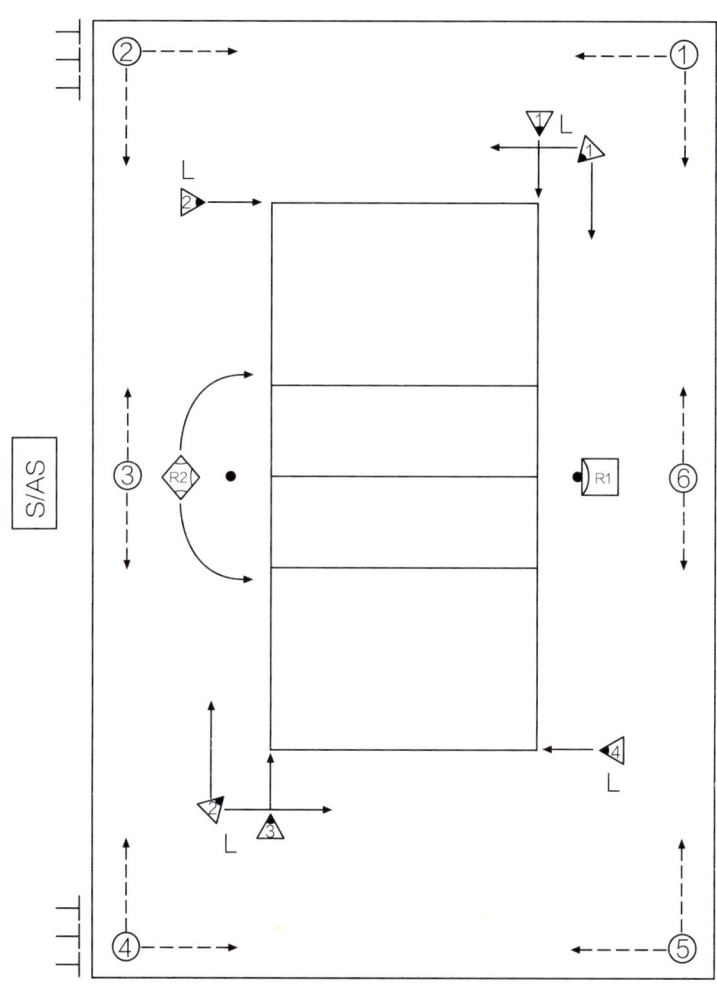

- ◧R1 = 第 1 裁判员
- ◇R2 = 第 2 裁判员
- S/AS = 记录员 / 辅助记录员
- ▷ = 司线员（数量 1~4 或 1~2）
- ④ = 捡球员（数量 1~6）
- ⊣ = 平沙员

图 9: 裁判员法定手势

图示：　　第 1 裁判员 第 2 裁判员 依其常规职责必须出示手势的裁判员
　　　　　第 1 裁判员 第 2 裁判员 在该特殊场景中出示手势的裁判员

1	允许发球

相关规则：12.3, 21.2.1.1

挥动发球队一侧的手臂

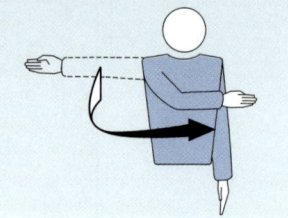

第 1 裁判员

2	发球队

相关规则：12.3, 21.2.3.1a, 21.2.3.2c, 21.2.3.3c

平举发球队一侧的手臂

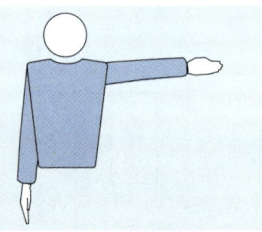

第 1 裁判员
第 2 裁判员

3	交换场区

相关规则：18.2, 23.2.5

两臂分别置于身体前后，屈肘平抬，绕身体转动

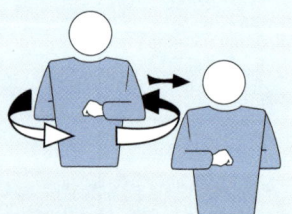

第 1 裁判员
第 2 裁判员

4	暂停

相关规则：15, 23.2.5

一臂屈肘抬起，将手掌放在另一侧前臂垂直立起的手指尖上（成 T 形），然后指出提出请求的队

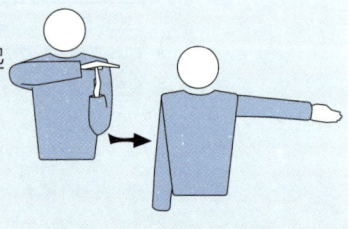

第 1 裁判员
第 2 裁判员

第二部分　比赛规则

| 5 | 不良行为警告 |

相关规则：20.1, 20.5
出示黄牌警告

第 1 裁判员

| 6 | 不良行为判罚 |

相关规则：20.3.1, 20.5
出示红牌判罚

第 1 裁判员

| 7 | 判罚出场 |

相关规则：20.3.2, 20.5
单手出示红、黄牌

第 1 裁判员

| 8 | 取消比赛资格 |

相关规则：20.3.3, 20.5
双手分持红、黄牌

第 1 裁判员

59

9	一局（或全场）比赛结束

相关规则：6.2, 6.3

双手展开，两臂在胸前交叉

第1裁判员

10	发球时球未抛起或离手

相关规则：12.4.1

一臂伸展上抬，掌心向上

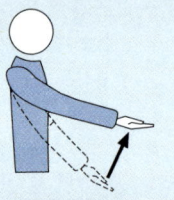

第1裁判员

11	发球延误

相关规则：12.4.4

一侧手上举，五指分开

第1裁判员

12	拦网犯规或掩护犯规

相关规则：12.5, 14.5, 14.6.3

两臂上举，掌心向前

第1裁判员

| 13 | 位置错误或轮转错误 |

相关规则：7.7.1, 12.6.1.1

一手食指在体前画圈

 第1裁判员
第2裁判员

| 14 | 界内球 |

相关规则：6.1.1.1, 8.3

一侧手臂和手指指向地面

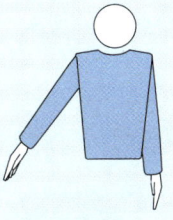

 第1裁判员
第2裁判员

| 15 | 界外球 |

相关规则：8.4.1, 8.4.2, 8.4.3, 8.4.4, 12.6.2.2, 13.2.2

双手展开，掌心向上，屈肘上举前臂

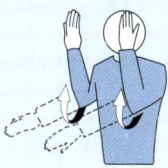

第1裁判员
第2裁判员

| 16 | 持球 |

相关规则：6.1.2, 9.3.3, 22.3.2.3b

一侧掌心向上，屈肘慢举前臂

第1裁判员

17 连击

相关规则：6.1.2, 9.1.1, 9.3.4, 22.3.2.3b

两手指分开，上举

第 1 裁判员

第 2 裁判员

18 四次击球

相关规则：9.3.1

四手指分开，上举

第 1 裁判员

19 队员触网犯规——发球时球触到标志杆之间的球网且没有越过球网的垂直平面

相关规则：12.6.2.1

对应一侧的手指向犯规一侧球网

第 1 裁判员

第 2 裁判员

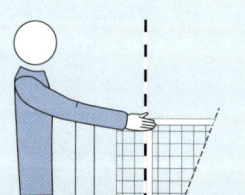

20 过网击球犯规

相关规则：11.4.1, 13.2.1

前臂置于球网上空，掌心向下

第 1 裁判员

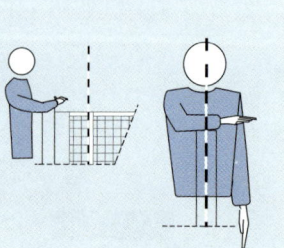

21　进攻性击球犯规

——队员张开手指完成进攻性击球或手指没有完全并拢吊球。
——对方发过来的球，队员在球的整体高于球网上沿时完成进攻性击球。
——队员用上手传球，且传球轨迹不垂直于双肩连线完成进攻性击球。队员试图传给同伴的球除外。

相关规则：13.2.3, 13.2.4, 13.2.5

一侧上臂举起，手展开，向下摆动前臂

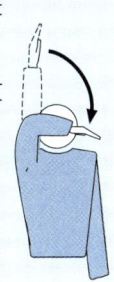

第1裁判员

22　队员由网下穿越进入对方场区和空间，干扰了对方比赛
球从球网下部完全通过球网
发球队员触及场地（包括端线）或发球区以外地面
在发球队员击球时，脚踏出比赛场区，发球队员除外

相关规则：8.4.5, 11.2.1, 12.4.3, 23.3.2.1, 23.3.2.6

手指指向网下或相应的线

第1裁判员
第2裁判员

23　双方犯规，重新进行

相关规则：6.1.2.2, 12.4.5

两臂屈肘，垂直抬起，竖起拇指

第1裁判员
第2裁判员

24　球触手出界

相关规则：14.6.4

两臂举起成垂直状，一手掌心轻擦另一手的指尖

第 1 裁判员

25　延误警告／延误判罚

相关规则：15.5.5, 16.2.2, 16.2.3

黄牌放在手腕上（警告）

红牌放在手腕上（判罚）

第 1 裁判员

警告　判罚

图 10: 司线员法定旗示

1　界内球

相关规则：8.3, 28.2.1.1
向下示旗

司线员

2　界外球

相关规则：8.4.1, 28.2.1.1
垂直向上示旗

司线员

3　触手出界

相关规则：28.2.1.2
将旗举起，旗顶部触到另一手掌心

司线员

4　球从非过网区通过，球触场外物体或发球时任何队员脚的犯规

相关规则：8.4.2, 8.4.3, 8.4.4, 12.4.3, 28.2.1.3, 28.2.1.4, 28.2.1.5, 28.2.1.6, 28.2.1.7
一手举起在头上晃动，另一手指向标志杆或相应一侧的端线

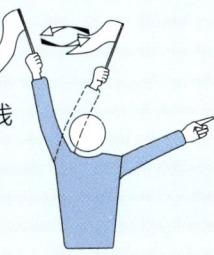

司线员

5	无法判断
	双臂胸前交叉
司线员	

第三部分

定义

第三部分 定义

赛前仪式

比赛开始前的一系列活动，包括：挑边、热身活动、根据技术手册的描述介绍运动队和裁判员。

比赛 / 控制区

比赛 / 控制区是围绕比赛场区和无障碍区的通道，直至外围的分界线或围栏。见图 1a。

区

区是比赛场地（即比赛场区和无障碍区）中规则赋予了特定目的（或专门的限制）的部分。区包括发球区和无障碍区。

网下空间

网下空间是球网及下网绳以下、两根网柱之间、地面以上的空间。

过网区

过网区的界限为：

——球网上端；

——两根标志杆及其延长线；

——顶棚。

球必须从过网区通过进入对方场区。

延伸空间

延伸空间是除过网区和网下空间之外的球网垂直空间。

国际排联特许

在特定的条件下,国际排联安排试用一些特殊器材、设备,目的在于推广沙滩排球运动或测试新的条件。

国际排联标准

国际排联向器材设备制造商提出的技术规格和要求。

犯规

a)违反规则的比赛行为。

b)违反规则的非比赛行为。

球队的第一次击球

以下三种情况中的比赛行为被视为球队的第 1 次击球:

— 接发球

— 接对方的进攻性击球

— 接被对方拦回的球

每球得分制

是每赢得一个回合即得 1 分的计分体系。

技术暂停

技术暂停是在正常暂停以外增加的强制性暂停,用于解说比赛和扩大商机,以推广沙滩排球运动。在国际排联比赛、世界性比赛和正式比赛中强制使用。

局间

两局之间的时间。第 3 局（决胜局）交换场区不能算作局间。

干扰比赛

给对方制造不利条件的任何行为或阻碍对方击球的任何行为。

场外物体

比赛场区以外或无障碍空间边缘附近的阻碍球飞行的人或物体。如：头顶的灯、裁判椅、电视设备、记录台和网柱等。场外物体不包括标志杆，因为标志杆被视为球网的一部分。

捡球员

捡球员的职责是在比赛过程之间将球滚向或提供给发球队员以保证比赛流畅进行。

平沙员

场地助理人员使用长沙耙或长杆平整场地上的沙，特别是场地界线和两根网柱之间中轴线附近的沙。

附：

本规则英文部分

说明：英文部分的页码沿用原文，详见其目录

OFFICIAL BEACH VOLLEYBALL RULES
2021-2024

Approved by the 37th FIVB World Congress 2021

Official Beach Volleyball Rules 2021-2024
Published by FIVB in 2021 – www.fivb.com
Design, layout and illustrations: © FIVB 2021

附：本规则英文部分

OFFICIAL BEACH VOLLEYBALL RULES
2021-2024

Approved by the 37th FIVB World Congress 2021

To be implemented in all competitions from 1st January 2022

CONTENTS

GAME CHARACTERISTICS	07
PART 1: PHILOSOPHY OF RULES AND REFEREEING	08
PART 2 – SECTION 1: GAME	11
CHAPTER 1 FACILITIES AND EQUIPMENT	12

1 PLAYING AREA 12
   1.1   DIMENSIONS 12
   1.2   PLAYING SURFACE 12
   1.3   LINES ON THE COURT 13
   1.4   ZONES AND AREAS 13
   1.5   WEATHER 13
   1.6   LIGHTING 13
2 NET AND POSTS 13
   2.1   HEIGHT OF THE NET 13
   2.2   STRUCTURE 14
   2.3   SIDE BANDS 14
   2.4   ANTENNAE 14
   2.5   POSTS 15
   2.6   ADDITIONAL EQUIPMENT 15
3 BALLS 15
   3.1   STANDARDS 15
   3.2   UNIFORMITY OF BALLS 15
   3.3   FOUR-BALL SYSTEM 15

| CHAPTER 2   PARTICIPANTS | 16 |

4 TEAMS 16
   4.1   TEAM COMPOSITION 16
   4.2   LOCATION OF THE TEAM 16
   4.3   EQUIPMENT 16
   4.4   CHANGE OF EQUIPMENT 17
   4.5   FORBIDDEN OBJECTS 17
5 TEAM LEADERS 17
   5.1   CAPTAIN 17

附：本规则英文部分

CHAPTER 3   PLAYING FORMAT   19

6   TO SCORE A POINT, TO WIN A SET AND THE MATCH 19
    6.1   TO SCORE A POINT 19
    6.2   TO WIN A SET 20
    6.3   TO WIN THE MATCH 20
    6.4   DEFAULT AND INCOMPLETE TEAM 20
7   STRUCTURE OF PLAY 20
    7.1   THE TOSS 20
    7.2   OFFICIAL WARM-UP SESSION 21
    7.3   TEAM LINE-UP 21
    7.4   POSITIONS 21
    7.5   POSITIONAL FAULT 21
    7.6   SERVICE ORDER 21
    7.7   SERVICE ORDER FAULT 21

CHAPTER 4   PLAYING ACTIONS   22

8   STATES OF PLAY 22
    8.1 BALL IN PLAY 22
    8.2 BALL OUT OF PLAY 22
    8.3 BALL "IN" 22
    8.4 BALL "OUT" 22
9   PLAYING THE BALL 22
    9.1   TEAM HITS 23
    9.2   CHARACTERISTICS OF THE HIT 23
    9.3   FAULTS IN PLAYING THE BALL 24
10   BALL AT THE NET 24
    10.1   BALL CROSSING THE NET 24
    10.2   BALL TOUCHING THE NET 25
    10.3   BALL IN THE NET 25
11   PLAYER AT THE NET 25
    11.1   REACHING BEYOND THE NET 25
    11.2   PENETRATION INTO THE OPPONENT'S SPACE, COURT AND/OR FREE ZONE 25
    11.3   CONTACT WITH THE NET 25
    11.4   PLAYER'S FAULTS AT THE NET 26
12   SERVICE 26
    12.1   FIRST SERVICE IN A SET 26
    12.2   SERVICE ORDER 26
    12.3   AUTHORIZATION OF THE SERVICE 27

12.4 EXECUTION OF THE SERVICE 27
12.5 SCREENING 27
12.6 FAULTS MADE DURING THE SERVICE 27
13 ATTACK HIT 28
13.1 CHARACTERISTICS OF THE ATTACK HIT 28
13.2 FAULTS OF THE ATTACK HIT 28
14 BLOCK 28
14.1 BLOCKING 28
14.2 BLOCK CONTACT 29
14.3 BLOCKING WITHIN THE OPPONENT'S SPACE 29
14.4 BLOCK AND TEAM HITS 29
14.5 BLOCKING THE SERVICE 29
14.6 BLOCKING FAULTS 29

CHAPTER 5   INTERRUPTIONS, DELAYS AND INTERVALS   30

15 INTERRUPTIONS 30
15.1 NUMBER OF REGULAR GAME INTERRUPTIONS 30
15.2 SEQUENCE OF REGULAR GAME INTERRUPTIONS 30
15.3 REQUEST FOR REGULAR GAME INTERRUPTIONS 30
15.4 TIME-OUTS AND TECHNICAL TIME-OUTS 30
15.5 IMPROPER REQUESTS. 31
16 GAME DELAYS 31
16.1 TYPES OF DELAYS 31
16.2 DELAY SANCTIONS 31
17 EXCEPTIONAL GAME INTERRUPTIONS 32
17.1 INJURY/ ILLNESS 32
17.2 EXTERNAL INTERFERENCE 32
17.3 PROLONGED INTERRUPTIONS 32
18 INTERVALS AND CHANGE OF COURTS/SWITCHES 33
18.1 INTERVALS 33
18.2 COURT SWITCHES 33

CHAPTER 6   PARTICIPANTS' CONDUCT   34

19 REQUIREMENTS OF CONDUCT 34
19.1 SPORTSMANLIKE CONDUCT 34
19.2 FAIR PLAY 34
20 MISCONDUCT AND ITS SANCTIONS 34
20.1 MINOR MISCONDUCT 34

20.2 MISCONDUCT LEADING TO SANCTIONS 35
20.3 SANCTION SCALE 35
20.4 MISCONDUCT BEFORE AND BETWEEN SETS 35
20.5 SUMMARY OF MISCONDUCT AND CARDS USED 36

PART 2 – SECTION 2: THE REFEREES, THEIR RESPONSIBILITIES AND OFFICIAL HAND SIGNALS 37

CHAPTER 7 REFEREES 38

21 REFEREEING TEAM AND PROCEDURES 38
   21.1 COMPOSITION 38
   21.2 PROCEDURES 38
22 1st REFEREE 39
   22.1 LOCATION 39
   22.2 AUTHORITY 39
   22.3 RESPONSIBILITIES 40
23 2nd REFEREE 40
   23.1 LOCATION 40
   23.2 AUTHORITY 40
   23.3 RESPONSIBILITIES 41
24 CHALLENGE REFEREE 42
   24.1 LOCATION 42
   24.2 RESPONSIBILITIES 42
25 RESERVE REFEREE 42
   25.1 LOCATION 42
   25.2 RESPONSIBILITIES 42
26 SCORER 43
   26.1 LOCATION 43
   26.2 RESPONSIBILITIES 43
27 ASSISTANT SCORER 44
   27.1 LOCATION 44
   27.2 RESPONSIBILITIES 44
28 LINE JUDGES 44
   28.1 LOCATION 44
   28.2 RESPONSIBILITIES 45
29 OFFICIAL SIGNALS 45
   29.1 REFEREES' HAND SIGNALS 45
   29.2 LINE JUDGES' FLAG SIGNALS 45

PART 2 – SECTION 3: DIAGRAMS   47
- D1   THE PLAYING AREA 48
- D2   THE PLAYING COURT 49
- D3   DESIGN OF THE NET 50
- D4a BALL CROSSING THE VERTICAL PLANE OF THE NET TO THE OPPONENT COURT 51
- D4b BALL CROSSING THE VERTICAL PLANE OF THE NET TO THE OPPONENT FREE ZONE ... 52
- D5   SCREEN 53
- D6   COMPLETED BLOCK 53
- D7   DETERRENTS AND SANCTIONS 54
       D7a MISCONDUCT WARNING AND SANCTIONS SCALE AND THEIR CONSEQUENCES 54
       D7b DELAY SANCTIONS SCALE AND CONSEQUENCES 54
- D8   LOCATION OF REFEREEING TEAM AND THEIR ASSISTANTS 55
- D9   REFEREES' OFFICIAL HAND SIGNALS 56-62
- D10 LINE JUDGES' OFFICIAL FLAG SIGNALS 63-64

PART 3: DEFINITIONS   65

INDEX   68

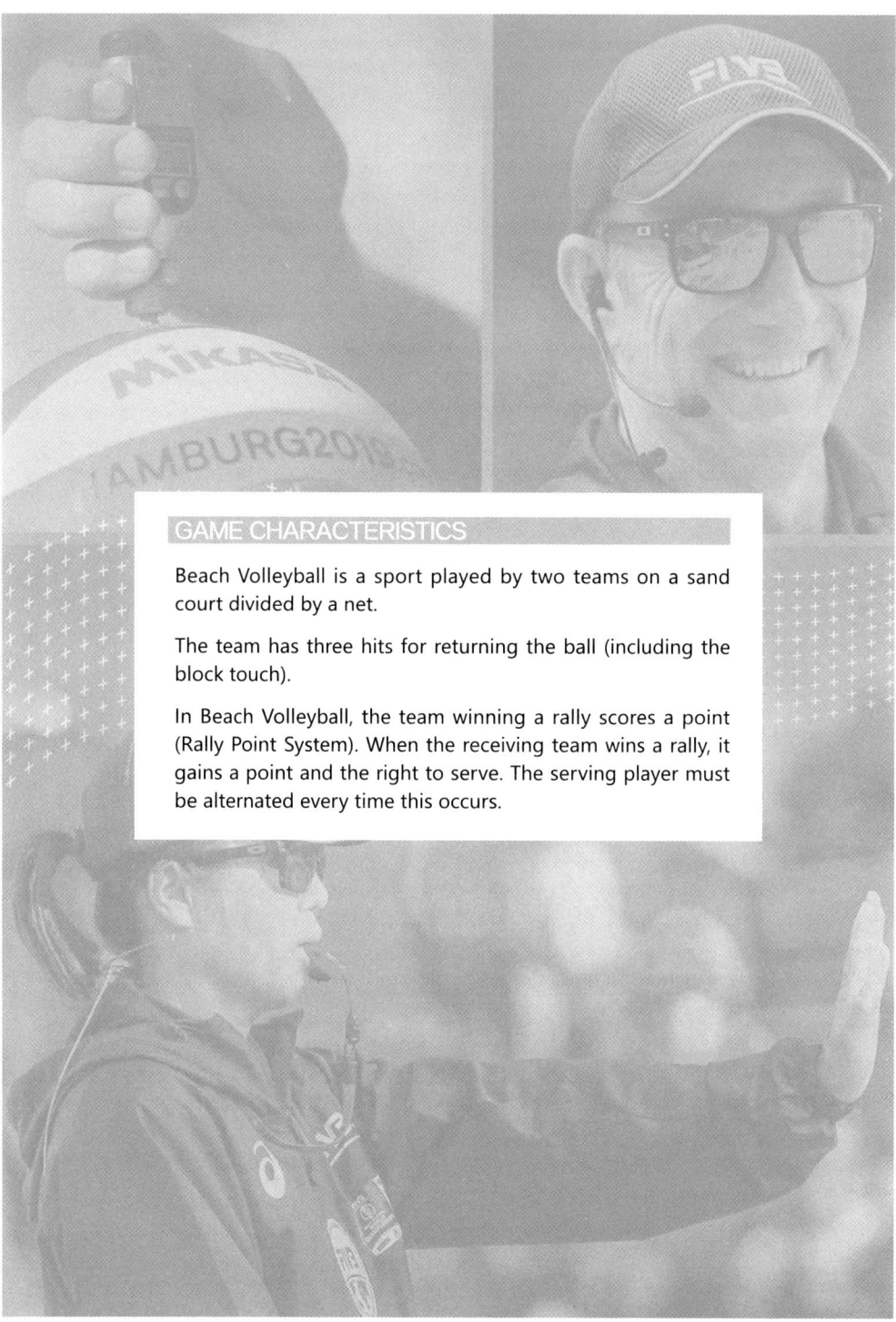

GAME CHARACTERISTICS

Beach Volleyball is a sport played by two teams on a sand court divided by a net.

The team has three hits for returning the ball (including the block touch).

In Beach Volleyball, the team winning a rally scores a point (Rally Point System). When the receiving team wins a rally, it gains a point and the right to serve. The serving player must be alternated every time this occurs.

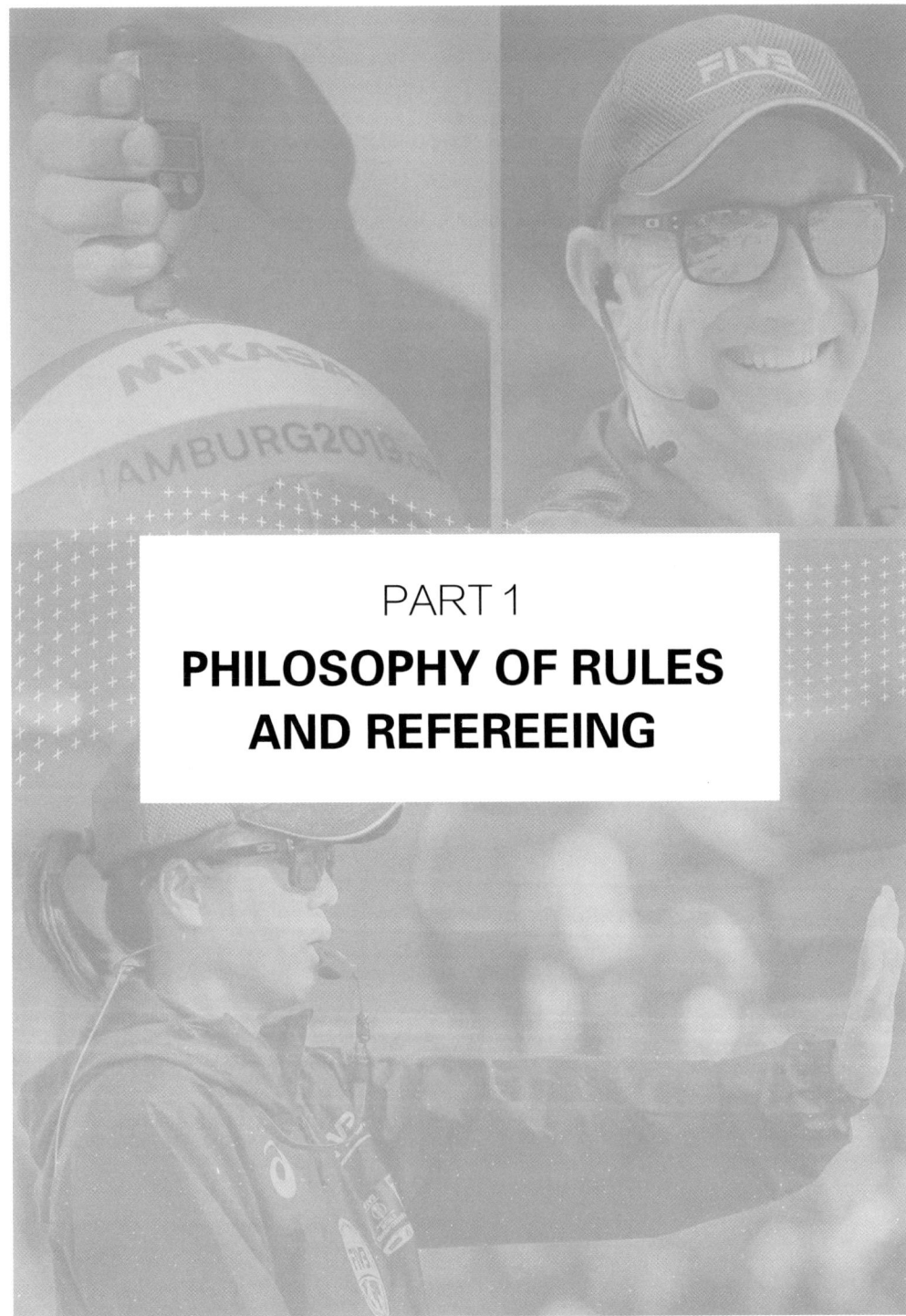

PART 1
PHILOSOPHY OF RULES AND REFEREEING

INTRODUCTION

By every measure, Beach Volleyball is one of the world's most successful and popular sports – it has larger TV viewing figures, larger followers on social media, greater (and growing) numbers of registered and recreational players, than almost any other sport, and an image which is dynamic, clean and colorful, combining, especially at the competitive levels, a visual and audible feast to satisfy every palate.

Put simply, it is **fast**, it is **exciting** and the action is **explosive**. Yet the Beach form of Volleyball comprises several crucial overlapping elements whose complimentary **interactions** render it unique amongst rally games, and create a special charm to differentiate it from other forms of the sport.

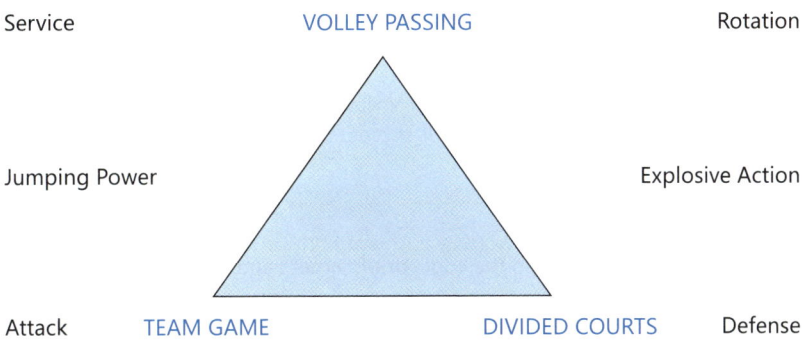

FIVB BEACH VOLLEYBALL IS A COMPETITIVE SPORT

Competition taps latent strengths. It exhibits the best of ability, spirit, creativity and aesthetics. The rules are structured to allow all of these qualities. The game's early exponents on the sands of California would still recognize it. Yet, in recent years the FIVB has made great strides in adapting the game to a modern audience.

In this regard, Beach Volleyball has retained certain distinctive and essential elements over the years. Some of these it shares with other net/ball/ racquet games: – Service – Rotation (taking turns to serve) – Attack – Defense – players able to play anywhere on court.

But the sport has moved on. Today it is more explosive, and more spectacular. It is fast and free flowing; it has athletic players doing sensational things on court in crowded venues. Additionally, Beach Volleyball is unique amongst net games in insisting that the ball is in constant flight – a flying ball – and by allowing each team a degree of internal passing before the ball must be returned to the opponents, creating a kind sharing of the ball to produce equal opportunities for scoring points. In recent years the FIVB has made a massive investment in the use of technology, with its Video Challenge System providing fairness to the efforts of the athletes, and encouraging philosophies which promote flowing play to entertain the public, both in the venue and on the screen. Competitors use this framework to contest techniques, tactics and power. The framework also allows players a freedom of expression to enthuse spectators and viewers, and create an unrivaled sporting spectacle.

And the image of Beach Volleyball is increasingly a good one as a consequence.

THE RULES TEXT

This text is aimed at a broad Beach Volleyball public – players, coaches, referees, spectators, commentators, and others – because an understanding of the rules allows better play and personal satisfaction – coaches can create better team structure and tactics, giving players full rein to display their skills. Additionally, an understanding of the relationship between written rules and actual actions on the court allows officials to make better decisions.

Beach Volleyball is both recreational and competitive. Recreational sport taps into the human spirit and promotes "fun" and healthy life. Competition allows people to exhibit the best of ability, creativity, freedom of expression and fighting spirit. The rules are designed and structured to allow all of these facets to flourish.

This introduction has at first focused on Beach Volleyball as a competitive sport, before setting out to identify the main qualities required for successful refereeing.

THE REFEREE WITHIN THIS FRAMEWORK

The essence of a good official lies in the concept of fairness and consistency:

Being positioned in the middle of both playing courts is a symbol of balance, encouraging the players to trust the referee's actions. However, the referee must be a facilitator rather than a controller, an orchestra director rather than a dictator, an efficient promoter rather than an "efficient" punisher.

By understanding the reason why a rule has been written and by being clear about its purpose within the framework of the "show", the referee becomes a big part of the overall successful production, while remaining largely in the background and intervening only when necessary. We can say that a good referee will use the rules to make the competition a fulfilling experience for all concerned.

To those who have read thus far, view the rules which follow as the current state of development of a great game, but keep in mind why these preceding few paragraphs may be of equal importance to you in your own position within the sport. So…

Get involved！
Keep the ball flying！
Understand the game！

附：本规则英文部分

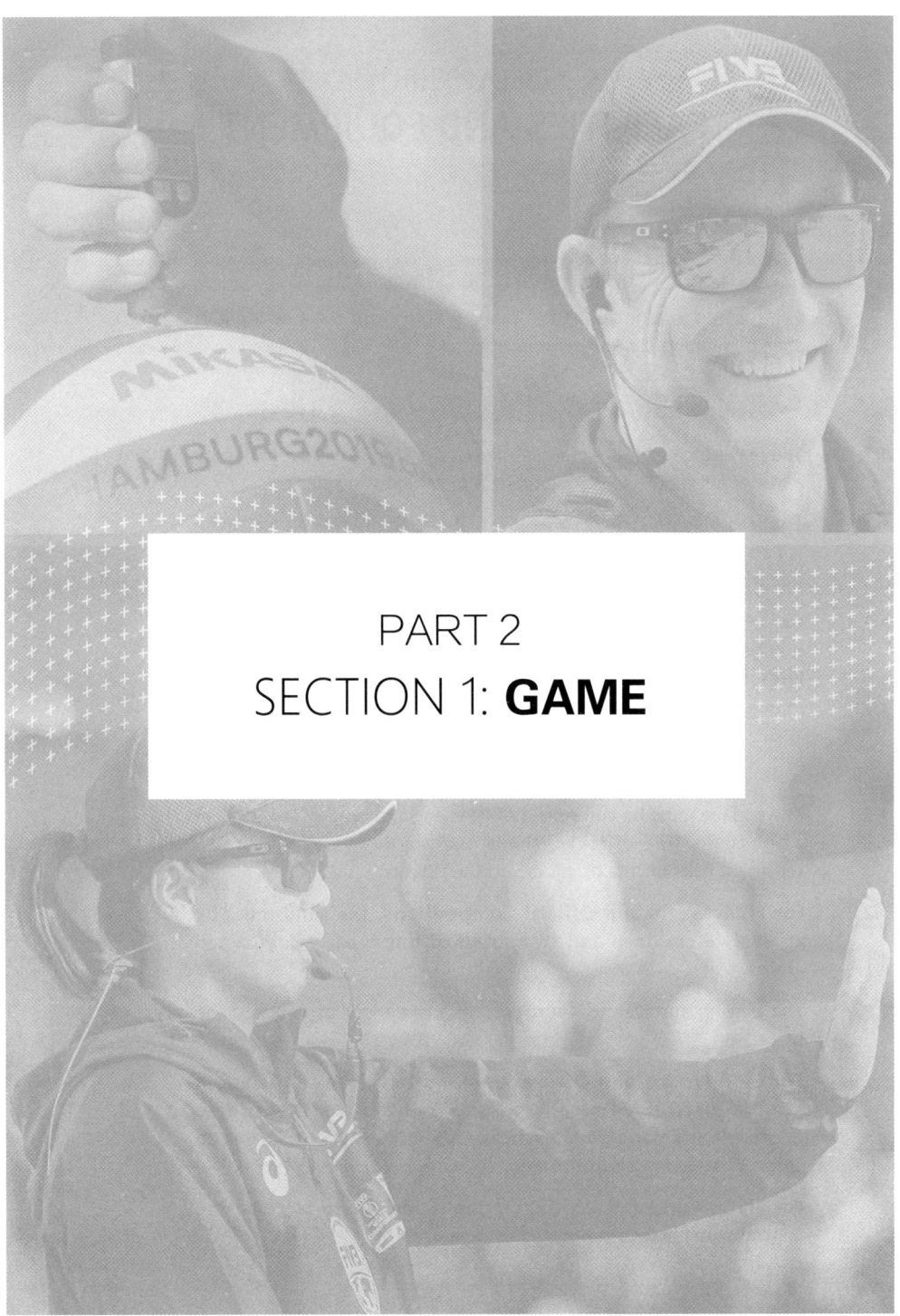

PART 2
SECTION 1: **GAME**

CHAPTER 1
FACILITIES AND EQUIPMENT

See Rules

1 PLAYING AREA

The playing area includes the playing court and the free zone. It shall be rectangular and symmetrical.

1.1, D1

1.1 DIMENSIONS

1.1.1 The playing court is a rectangle measuring 16 x 8 m, surrounded by a free zone, which is a minimum of 3 m wide on all sides.

D2

The free playing space is the space above the playing area, which is free from all obstructions. The free playing space shall measure a minimum of 7 m in height from the playing surface.

1.1.2 **For FIVB, World and Official Competitions, the free zone is a minimum of 5 m and a maximum of 6 m from the end lines/side lines. The free playing space shall measure a minimum of 12.5 m in height from the playing surface.**

1.2 PLAYING SURFACE

1.2.1 The surface must be composed of levelled sand, as flat and uniform as possible, free of rocks, shells and anything else which can represent risks of cuts or injuries to the players.

1.2.2 **For FIVB, World and Official Competitions, the sand must be at least 40 cm deep and composed of fine loosely compacted grains.**

1.2.3 The playing surface must not present any danger of injury to the players.

1.2.4 **For FIVB, World and Official Competitions, the sand should also be sifted to an acceptable size, not too coarse, and free of stones and dangerous particles. It should not be too fine to cause dust and stick to the skin.**

1.2.5 **For FIVB, World and Official Competitions, a tarp to cover the central court is recommended in case of rain.**

1.3 LINES ON THE COURT

1.3.1 All lines are 5 cm wide. The lines must be of a colour which contrasts sharply with the colour of the sand.

1.3.2 Boundary lines

Two side lines and two end lines mark the playing court. There is no centre line. Both side and end lines are placed inside the dimensions of the playing court.

Court lines should be ribbons made of a resistant material, and any exposed anchors should be of a soft, flexible material.

1.4 ZONES AND AREAS

There is only the playing court, service zone and the free zone surrounding the playing court.

1.4.1 The service zone is an 8 m wide area behind the end line, which extends to the edge of the free zone.

1.5 WEATHER

The weather must not present any danger of injury to the players.

1.6 LIGHTING

For FIVB, World and Official Competitions, played at night, the lighting on the playing area should be 1,000 to 1,500 lux measured at 1 m above the surface of the playing area.

2 NET AND POSTS

2.1 HEIGHT OF THE NET

2.1.1 Placed vertically over the middle of the court there is a net whose top is set at the height of 2.43 m for men and 2.24 m for women.

Note: The height of the net may be varied for specific age groups as follows:

Age Groups	Females	Males
16 years and under	2.24 m	2.24 m
14 years and under	2.12 m	2.12 m
12 years and under	2.00 m	2.00 m

2.1.2 Its height is measured from the centre of the playing court with a measuring rod. The net height (over the two side lines) must be exactly the same and must not exceed the official height by more than 2 cm.

2.2 STRUCTURE

The net is 8.5 m long and 1 m (+/- 3 cm) wide when it is hung taut, placed vertically over the narrow axis at the middle of the playing court.

D3

It is made of 10 cm square mesh. At its top and bottom there are two 7-10 cm wide horizontal bands made of two-fold canvas, preferably in dark blue or bright colours, sewn along its full length. Each extremity of the upper band has a hole through which passes a cord fastening the upper band to the posts to keep the top of the net stretched taut.

Within the bands, there is a flexible cable in the upper one and a cord in the bottom one for fastening the net to the posts and keeping its top and bottom taut. It is permissible to have advertising on the horizontal bands of the net.

For FIVB, World and Official Competitions, an 8.0 m net with smaller meshes and brandings displayed between the ends of the net and the posts may be used, provided that the visibility of the athletes and officials will be preserved. Publicity may be printed on the above items as per FIVB regulations.

2.3 SIDE BANDS

Two coloured bands, 5 cm wide (same width as the court lines) and 1 m long, are fastened vertically to the net and placed directly above each side line. They are considered as part of the net.

14.1.1, D3

Advertising is permitted on the side bands.

2.4 ANTENNAE

An antenna is a flexible rod, 1.80 m long and 10 mm in diameter, made of fibreglass or similar material.

An antenna is fastened at the outer edge of each side band. The antennae are placed on opposite sides of the net.

The top 80 cm of each antenna extends above the net and is marked with 10 cm stripes of contrasting colour, preferably red and white.

The antennae are considered as part of the net and laterally delimit the crossing space.

附：本规则英文部分

2.5 POSTS D2, D3

2.5.1 The posts supporting the net are placed at a distance of 0.70-1.00 m outside each side line. They are 2.55 m high and preferably adjustable.

For FIVB, World and Official Competitions, the posts supporting the net are placed at a distance of 1 m outside the side lines.

2.5.2 The posts are rounded and smooth, fixed to the ground without wires. There shall be no dangerous or obstructing devices. Posts must be padded.

2.6 ADDITIONAL EQUIPMENT

All additional equipment is determined by FIVB regulations.

3 BALLS

3.1 STANDARDS 3.2

The ball shall be spherical, made of a flexible material (leather, synthetic leather, or similar) which does not absorb moisture, i.e. more suitable to outdoor conditions since matches can be played when it is raining. The ball has a bladder inside made of rubber or a similar material. Approval of synthetic leather material is determined by FIVB regulations.

Colour: light uniform colour or a combination of colours.

Circumference: 66 to 68 cm.

Weight: 260 to 280 g.

Inside pressure: 0.175 to 0.225 kg/cm2 (171 to 221 mbar or hPa).

3.2 UNIFORMITY OF BALLS

All balls used in a match must have the same standards regarding circumference, weight, pressure, type, colour, etc.

FIVB, World and Official Competitions must be played with FIVB approved balls, unless by agreement of FIVB. 3.1, 23.2.8

3.3 FOUR-BALL SYSTEM

For FIVB, World and Official Competitions, four balls shall be used. In this case, six ball retrievers are stationed one at each corner of the free zone and one behind each referee. D8

CHAPTER 2
PARTICIPANTS

See Rules

4 TEAMS

4.1 TEAM COMPOSITION

4.1.1 A team is composed exclusively of two players.

4.1.2 Only the two players recorded on the score sheet have the right to participate in the match.

4.1.3 One of the players is the team captain who shall be indicated on the score sheet.

4.1.4 **For FIVB, World and Official Competitions, players are not allowed to receive external assistance or coaching during a match (Exceptions: see Specific Regulations for Age Competitions and for Phases 1 and 2 of the Continental Cup).**

4.2 LOCATION OF THE TEAM

The team's areas (including two chairs each) must be 5 m from the sideline, and no closer than 3 m from the scorer's table.

4.3 EQUIPMENT

A player's equipment consists of shorts or a bathing suit. A jersey or "tank-top" is optional except when specified in Tournament Regulations. Players may wear a hat/head covering.

4.1.1

4.3.1 **For FIVB, World and Official Competitions, players of a given team must wear uniforms of the same colour and style according to tournament regulations. Player's uniforms must be clean.**

4.3.2 Players must play barefoot except when authorized by the 1st referee.

4.3.3 Players' jerseys (or shorts if players are allowed to play without shirt) must be numbered 1 and 2.

4.3.3.1 The number must be placed on the chest (or on the front of the shorts).

4.3.3.2 The number must be of a contrasting colour to the jersey and a minimum of 10 cm in height. The stripe forming the number shall be a minimum of 1.5 cm wide.

4.4　CHANGE OF EQUIPMENT

If both teams arrive at a match dressed in jerseys of the same colour, a toss shall be conducted to determine which team shall change.

The first referee may authorize one or more players:

4.4.1	to play with socks and/or shoes,	
4.4.2	to change wet jerseys between sets provided that the new ones also follow tournament and FIVB regulations.	4.3.3
4.4.3	If requested by a player, the first referee may authorize him/her to play with an undershirt and training pants.	

4.5　FORBIDDEN OBJECTS

4.5.1　It is forbidden to wear objects which may cause injury or give an artificial advantage to the player.

4.5.2　Players may wear glasses or lenses at their own risk.

4.5.3　Compression pads (padded injury protection devices) may be worn for protection or support.

For FIVB, World and Official Competitions for seniors, these devices or visible underwear must be of the same colour as part of the uniform.

Black, white or neutral colours may be also used provided that all using players wear the same colour.

5　TEAM LEADERS

The team captain is responsible for maintaining team conduct and discipline.

5.1　CAPTAIN

5.1.1　PRIOR TO THE MATCH, the team captain:

a) Signs the score sheet.

b) Represents his/her team in the toss.

5.1.2	During the match, only the captain is authorized to speak to the referees while the ball is out of play in the following three cases:	8.2
5.1.2.1	to ask for an explanation on the application or interpretation of the Rules; if the explanation does not satisfy the captain, the captain must immediately inform the 1st referee of his/her wish to Protest;	

5.1.2.2 to ask authorization:

    a) to change uniforms or equipment,
    b) to verify the number of the serving player,
    c) to check the net, the ball, the surface etc.,
    d) to realign a court line;

5.1.2.3 to request time-outs.   15.2.1, 15.4.1

    Note: the players must have authorization from the referees to leave the playing area.

5.1.3 **AT THE END OF THE MATCH:**

5.1.3.1 Both players thank the referees and the opponents. The Captain signs the score sheet to ratify the result;

5.1.3.2 If the captain previously requested a Protest Protocol via the 1st referee and this has not been successfully resolved at the time of the occurrence, he/she has the right to confirm it as a formal written protest, recorded on the score sheet at the end of the match.   5.1.2.1

附：本规则英文部分

CHAPTER 3
PLAYING FORMAT

See Rules

6 TO SCORE A POINT, TO WIN A SET AND THE MATCH

6.1 TO SCORE A POINT

6.1.1　Point

A team scores a point:

6.1.1.1　by successfully landing the ball on the opponent's court;　D9 (14)

6.1.1.2　when the opponent team commits a fault;

6.1.1.3　when the opponent team receives a penalty.

6.1.2　Fault

A team commits a fault by making a playing action contrary to the rules (or by violating them in some other way). The referees judge the faults and determine the consequences according to the rules:

6.1.2.1　if two or more faults are committed successively, only the first one is counted;

6.1.2.2　if two or more faults are committed by opponents simultaneously, a DOUBLE FAULT is called and the rally is replayed.　D9 (23)

6.1.3　Rally and completed rally

A **rally** is the sequence of playing actions from the moment of the service hit by the server until the ball is out of play. A **completed rally** is the sequence of playing actions which results in the award of a point. This includes:

8.1, 8.2,
12.2.2.1,
12.4.4,
22.3.2.2

– **the award of a penalty**
– **loss of service for a service hit made after the time-limit.**

6.1.3.1　If the serving team wins a rally, it scores a point and continues to serve.

6.1.3.2　If the receiving team wins a rally, it scores a point and it must serve next.

19

6.2 TO WIN A SET

A set (except the deciding 3rd set) is won by the team which first scores 21 points with a minimum lead of two points. In the case of a 20-20 tie, play is continued until a two-point lead is achieved (22-20; 23-21; etc).

D9 (9)

6.3 TO WIN THE MATCH

6.3.1 The match is won by the team that wins two sets.

D9 (9)

6.3.2 In the case of a 1-1 tie, the deciding 3rd set is played to 15 points with a minimum lead of 2 points.

6.4 DEFAULT AND INCOMPLETE TEAM

6.4.1 If a team refuses to play after being summoned to do so, it is declared in default and forfeits the match with the result 0-2 for the match and 0-21, 0-21 for each set.

6.4.2 A team that does not appear on the playing court on time is declared in default.

6.4.1

6.4.3 A team that is declared INCOMPLETE for the set or for the match, loses the set or the match. The opponent team is given the points, or the points and the sets, needed to win the set or the match. The incomplete team keeps its points and sets.

6.2, 6.3, 7.3.1

For FIVB, World and Official Competitions, whenever the Pool Play format is implemented, Rule 6.4 above may be subject to modifications as stated in the Specific Competition Regulations issued by the FIVB in due time, establishing the modality to be followed for treating the default and incomplete team cases.

7 STRUCTURE OF PLAY

7.1 THE TOSS

Before the official warm up, the 1st referee conducts the toss to decide upon the first service and the sides of the court in the first set.

7.1.1 The toss is taken in the presence of the two team captains, where appropriate.

7.1.2 The winner of the toss chooses:

EITHER

7.1.2.1 the right to serve or to receive the service,

OR

7.1.2.2	the side of the playing court.

The loser takes the remaining choice.

7.1.2.3	In the second set the loser of the toss in the first set will have the choice of 7.1.2.1 or 7.1.2.2.

A new toss will be conducted for the deciding set.

7.2 OFFICIAL WARM-UP SESSION

Prior to the match, if the teams have previously had another playing court at their disposal, they will have a 3-minute official warm-up period at the net; if not, they may have 5 minutes.

7.3 TEAM LINE-UP

7.3.1	Both players of each team must always be in play.	4.1.1

7.4 POSITIONS

At the moment the ball is hit by the server, each team must be within its own court (except the server).

7.4.1	The players are free to position themselves. There are NO determined positions on the court.

7.5 POSITIONAL FAULT

7.5.1	There are NO positional order faults.

7.6 SERVICE ORDER

7.6.1	Service order must be maintained throughout the set (as determined by the team captain immediately following the toss).
7.6.2	When the receiving team has gained the right to serve, its players "rotate" one position.

7.7 SERVICE ORDER FAULT

7.7.1	A service order fault is committed when the service is not made according to the service order. The team is sanctioned with a point and service to the opponent.	D9 (13)
7.7.2	The scorer(s) must correctly indicate the service order and correct any incorrect server prior to the whistle for service.	

CHAPTER 4
PLAYING ACTIONS

		See Rules
8	**STATES OF PLAY**	

8.1 BALL IN PLAY

The ball is in play from the moment of the hit of the service authorized by the 1st referee.

12, 12.3

8.2 BALL OUT OF PLAY

The ball is out of play at the moment of the fault which is whistled by one of the referees; in the absence of a fault, at the moment of the whistle.

8.3 BALL "IN"

The ball is "in" if at any moment of its contact with the playing surface, some part of the ball touches the court, including touching the boundary lines.

D9 (14), D10 (1)

8.4 BALL "OUT"

The ball is "out" when it:

8.4.1	falls on the ground completely outside the boundary lines (without touching them);	1.3.2, D9 (15), D10 (2)
8.4.2	touches an object outside the court, or a person out of play;	D9 (15), D10 (4)
8.4.3	touches the antennae, ropes, posts or the net itself outside the side bands;	2.3, D3, D4a, D9 (15), D10 (4)
8.4.4	crosses the vertical plane of the net either partially or totally outside the crossing space during service or during the third hit of the team (exception: Rule 10.1.2).	2.3, 10.1.2, D4a, D9 (15), D10 (4)
8.4.5	crosses completely the lower space under the net.	D4a, D9 (22)

9	**PLAYING THE BALL**	

Each team must play within its own playing area and playing space

10.1.2

(except Rule 10.1.2).

The ball may, however, be retrieved from beyond its own free zone and over the scoring table in its complete extension.

9.1 TEAM HITS

A hit is any contact with the ball by a player in play.

Each team is entitled to a maximum of three hits for returning the ball over the net. If more are used, the team commits the fault of "FOUR HITS".

These team hits include not only intentional hits by the player, but also unintentional contacts with the ball.

9.1.1 CONSECUTIVE CONTACTS

A player may not hit the ball two times consecutively (exceptions, see Rules: 9.2.2.2, 9.2.2.3, 14.2 and 14.4.2).   9.2.2.1, 14.2, 14.4.2, D9 (17)

9.1.2 SIMULTANEOUS CONTACTS

Two players may touch the ball at the same moment.

9.1.2.1 When two teammates touch the ball simultaneously, it is counted as two hits (with the exception of blocking).   14.2

If they reach for the ball but only one of them touches it, one hit is counted.

If players collide, no fault is committed.

9.1.2.2 When two opponents touch the ball simultaneously over the net and the ball remains in play, the team receiving the ball is entitled to another three hits. If such a ball goes "out", it is the fault of the team on the opposite side.

9.1.2.3 If simultaneous hits by two opponents over the net lead to an extended contact with the ball, play continues.   9.1.2.2

9.1.2.4 If the ball hits the antenna after simultaneous hits by two opponents over the net, the rally should be replayed.

9.1.3 ASSISTED HIT

Within the playing area, a player is not permitted to take support from a teammate or any structure/object in order to hit the ball.

However, a player who is about to commit a fault (touch the net or interfere with an opponent, etc.) may be stopped or held back by a team-mate.

9.2 CHARACTERISTICS OF THE HIT

9.2.1 The ball may touch any part of the body.

9.2.2	The ball must not be caught or thrown. It can rebound in any direction.	9.3.3
9.2.2.1	Simultaneous Contacts:	9.2.1
	The ball may touch various parts of the body, provided that the contacts take place simultaneously.	
9.2.2.2	Consecutive contacts:	9.3.4
	At the first hit of the team, provided it is not made overhand with fingers, consecutive contacts are permitted provided that the contacts occur during one action. During the first hit of the team if it is played overhand using fingers, the ball may NOT contact the fingers/ hands consecutively, even if the contacts occur during one action.	
9.2.2.3	However, at blocking, consecutive contacts may be made by one or more players, provided that they occur during one action;	14.2
9.2.2.4	Extended contacts:	
	In defensive action of a hard driven ball, the ball contact can be extended momentarily even if an overhand finger action is used.	

9.3 FAULTS IN PLAYING THE BALL

9.3.1	FOUR HITS: a team hits the ball four times before returning it.	9.1, D9 (18)
9.3.2	ASSISTED HIT: a player takes support from a teammate or any structure/object in order to hit the ball within the playing area.	9.1.3
9.3.3	CATCH: the ball is caught and/or thrown; it does not rebound from the hit. (Exceptions 9.2.2.1, 9.2.2.2).	9.2.2, D9 (16)
9.3.4	DOUBLE CONTACT: a player hits the ball twice in succession or the ball contacts various parts of his/her body in succession.	9.1.1, 9.2.2.2, D9 (17)

10 BALL AT THE NET

10.1 BALL CROSSING THE NET

10.1.1	The ball sent to the opponent's court must go over the net within the crossing space. The crossing space is the part of the vertical plane of the net limited as follows:	D4a
10.1.1.1	below, by the top of the net;	
10.1.1.2	at the sides, by the antennae, and their imaginary extension;	
10.1.1.3	above, by the ceiling or structure (if any).	
10.1.2	The ball that has crossed the net plane to the opponent's free zone totally or partly through the external space, may be played back within the team hits, provided that:	9.1, D4b

10.1.2.1	The ball when played back crosses the vertical plane of the net again totally, or partly through the external space on the same side of the court.	D4b
	The opponent team may not prevent such action.	
10.1.3	The ball is "out" when it crosses completely the lower space under the net.	
10.1.4	A player, however, may enter the opponents' court in order to play the ball before it passes outside the crossing space, or before it crosses completely the lower space.	10.1.3

10.2 BALL TOUCHING THE NET

	While crossing the net, the ball may touch it.	10.1.1

10.3 BALL IN THE NET

10.3.1	A ball driven into the net may be recovered within the limits of the three team hits.	9.1
10.3.2	If the ball rips the mesh of the net or tears it down, the rally is cancelled and replayed.	

11 PLAYER AT THE NET

11.1 REACHING BEYOND THE NET

11.1.1	In blocking, a player may touch the ball beyond the net, provided that he/she does not interfere with the opponent's play, before the latter's attack hit.	14.1, 14.3
11.1.2	After an attack hit, a player is permitted to pass his/her hand beyond the net, provided that the contact has been made within his/her own playing space.	

11.2 PENETRATION INTO THE OPPONENT'S SPACE, COURT AND/OR FREE ZONE

11.2.1	A player may enter into the opponent's space, court and/or free zone, provided that this does not interfere with the opponent's play.	10.1.4

11.3 CONTACT WITH THE NET

11.3.1	Contact with the net by a player between the antennae, during the action of playing the ball, is a fault.	11.4.3, 22.3.2.3.c, 26.3.2.2, D3
	The action of playing the ball includes (among others) take-off, hit (or attempt) and landing safely, ready for a new action.	

11.3.2	Players may touch the post, ropes, or any other object outside the antennae, including the net itself, provided that it does not interfere with the play (except Rule 9.1.3).	
11.3.3	When the ball is driven into the net, causing it to touch an opponent, no fault is committed.	

11.4 PLAYER'S FAULTS AT THE NET

11.4.1	A player touches the ball or an opponent in the opponent's space before or during the opponent's attack hit.	D9 (20)
11.4.2	A player interferes with the opponent's play while penetrating into the opponent's space under the net.	
11.4.3	A player interferes with play by (amongst others):	11.3.1, D3

– touching the net between the antennae or the antenna itself during his/her action of playing the ball;

– using the net between the antennae as a support or stabilizing aid

– creating an unfair advantage over the opponent by touching the net

– making actions which hinder an opponent's legitimate attempt to play the ball;

– catching/holding on to the net.

Any player close to the ball as it is played, and who is him/herself trying to play it, is considered in the action of playing the ball, even if no contact is made with it.

However, touching the net outside the antenna is not to be considered as a fault (except for Rule 9.1.3).

12 SERVICE

The service is the act of putting the ball into play by the correct serving player placed in the service zone.

12.1 FIRST SERVICE IN A SET

12.1.1	The first service of a set is executed by the team determined by the toss.	6.3.2, 7.1

12.2 SERVICE ORDER

12.2.1	The players must follow the service order recorded on the score sheet.
12.2.2	After the first service in a set, the player to serve is determined as follows:
12.2.2.1	when the serving team wins the rally, the player who served before, serves again.

12.2.2.2	when the receiving team wins the rally, it gains the right to serve and the player who did not serve last time will serve.	

12.3 AUTHORIZATION OF THE SERVICE

	The 1st referee authorizes the service, after having checked that both teams are ready to play and that the server is in possession of the ball.	D9 (1)

12.4 EXECUTION OF THE SERVICE

12.4.1	The ball shall be hit with one hand or any part of the arm after being tossed or released from the hand(s).	D9 (10)
12.4.2	Only one toss or release of the ball is allowed. Moving the ball in the hands is permitted.	
12.4.3	The server may move freely within the service zone. At the moment of the service hit or take-off for a jump service, the server must not touch the court (the end line included) or the ground outside the service zone. His/her foot may not go under the end line.	1.4.2, D9 (22), D10 (4)
	After the hit, he/she may step or land outside the service zone, or inside the court. If the line moves because of the sand pushed by the server, it is not considered a fault.	
12.4.4	The server must hit the ball within 5 seconds after the 1st referee whistles for service.	D9 (11)
12.4.5	A service executed before the referee's whistle is cancelled and repeated.	D9 (23)
12.4.6	If the ball, after having been tossed or released by the server, lands without being touched or caught by the server, it is considered as a service.	
12.4.7	No further service attempt will be permitted.	

12.5 SCREENING

		D9 (12)
12.5.1	A player of the serving team must not prevent the opponent, through individual screening, from seeing the service hit AND the flight path of the ball.	D5
12.5.2	A player of the serving team makes a screen by waving arms, jumping or moving sideways during the execution of the service, in order that both the service hit and the flight path of the ball are hidden until the ball reaches the vertical plane of the net. Should either be visible to the receiving team this is not a screen.	D5

12.6 FAULTS MADE DURING THE SERVICE

12.6.1 Serving faults

The following faults lead to a change of service. The server:

12.6.1.1	violates the service order,	12.2, D9 (13)
12.6.1.2	does not execute the service properly.	12.4
12.6.2	Faults after the service hit	
	After the ball has been correctly hit, the service becomes a fault if the ball:	
12.6.2.1	touches a player of the serving team or fails to cross the vertical plane of the net completely through the crossing space;	D9 (19)
12.6.2.2	goes "out" ;	8.4, D9 (15)
12.6.2.3	passes over a screen	D5

13　ATTACK HIT

13.1　CHARACTERISTICS OF THE ATTACK HIT

13.1.1	All actions which direct the ball towards the opponent, with the exception of service and block, are considered as attack hits.	
13.1.2	An attack-hit is completed the moment the ball completely crosses the vertical plane of the net or is touched by an opponent.	
13.1.3	Any player may carry out an attack-hit at any height, provided that his/her contact with the ball has been made within the player's own playing space (except Rule 13.2.4, 13.2.5 below).	13.2.4, 13.2.5

13.2　FAULTS OF THE ATTACK HIT

13.2.1	A player hits the ball within the playing space of the opposing team.	13.1.2, D9 (20)
13.2.2	A player hits the ball "out" .	8.4, D9 (15)
13.2.3	A player completes an attack-hit using an open-handed finger action or if using finger tips that are not rigid and together.	D9 (21)
13.2.4	A player completes an attack hit on the opponent's service, when the ball is entirely higher than the top of the net.	D9 (21)
13.2.5	A player completes an attack-hit using an overhand pass which has a trajectory not perpendicular to the line of the shoulders. The exception is when the player is attempting to set to his or her teammate.	D9 (21)

14　BLOCK

14.1　BLOCKING

14.1.1　Blocking is the action of players close to the net to intercept the ball coming from the opponent by reaching higher than the top of the net, regardless of the height of the ball contact. At the moment of the contact with the ball, a part of the body must be higher than the top of the net.

14.1.2 Block Attempt

A block attempt is the action of blocking without touching the ball.

14.1.3 Completed Block

A block is completed whenever the ball is touched by a blocker.   D6

14.1.4 Collective Block

A collective block is executed by two players close to each other, and is completed when one of them touches the ball.

14.2　BLOCK CONTACT

Consecutive (quick and continuous) contacts may occur by one or more blockers provided that the contacts are made during one action. These are counted as only one team hit. These contacts may occur with any part of the body.   9.1.1, 9.2.3

14.3　BLOCKING WITHIN THE OPPONENT'S SPACE

In blocking, the player may place his/her hands and arms beyond the net, provided that this action does not interfere with the opponent's play. Thus, it is not permitted to touch the ball beyond the net before an opponent has executed an attack hit.   13.1.1

14.4　BLOCK AND TEAM HITS

14.4.1 A blocking contact is counted as a team hit. The blocking team will have only two more hits after a blocking contact.

14.4.2 The first hit after the block may be executed by any player, including the one who has touched the ball during the block.

14.5　BLOCKING THE SERVICE   D9 (12)

To block an opponent's service is forbidden.

14.6　BLOCKING FAULTS

14.6.1 The blocker touches the ball in the OPPONENT'S space before the opponent's attack hit.   14.3, D9 (20)

14.6.2 Blocking the ball in the opponent's space from outside the antenna.

14.6.3 A player blocks the opponent's service.   D9 (12)

14.6.4 The ball is sent "out" off the block.   D9 (24)

CHAPTER 5
INTERRUPTIONS, DELAYS AND INTERVALS

See Rules

15 INTERRUPTIONS

An interruption is the time between one completed rally and the 1st referee's whistle for the next service.

The only **regular game** interruptions are TIME-OUTS. D9 (4)

15.1 NUMBER OF REGULAR GAME INTERRUPTIONS

Each team may request a maximum of one time-out per set.

15.2 SEQUENCE OF REGULAR GAME INTERRUPTIONS

15.2.1 Request for time-out by both teams may follow one another, within the same interruption.

15.2.2 There are no substitutions.

15.2.3 It is not permited to request any regular game interruption after having had a request rejected and sanctioned by a delay warning during the same interruption (i.e. before the end of next completed rally).

15.3 REQUEST FOR REGULAR GAME INTERRUPTIONS

Regular game interruptions may be requested only by the captain.

15.4 TIME-OUTS AND TECHNICAL TIME-OUTS

15.4.1 Time-out requests must be made by showing the corresponding hand signal, when the ball is out of play and before the whistle for service. All requested time-outs last for 30 seconds. D9 (4)

15.4.2 **For FIVB, World and Official Competitions, in sets 1 and 2, one additional 30-second "Technical Time-Out" is applied automatically when the sum of the points scored by the teams equals 21 points. The lenght of the Time-Outs and Technical Time-Outs could be adjusted if the FIVB approves such request based on a request from the Organizer.**

15.4.3 In the deciding (3rd) set, there are no "Technical Time-Outs" ; only one time-out of 30 seconds duration may be requested by each team.

15.4.4	During all regular interruptions (including Technical Time Outs) and set intervals, players must go to the designated players' area.	15.5, 16.1

15.5 IMPROPER REQUESTS

Among others, it is improper to request a time-out:

15.5.1	during a rally or at the moment of, or after the whistle to serve,	6.1.3
15.5.2	by a non-authorised team member,	
15.5.3	after having exhausted the authorized time-outs.	15.1
15.5.4	Any further improper request in the same match by the same team constitutes a delay.	D9 (25)

16 GAME DELAYS

16.1 TYPES OF DELAYS

An improper action of a team that defers resumption of the game is a delay and includes, among others:

16.1.1	prolonging time-outs, after having been instructed to resume the game;	
16.1.2	repeating an improper request;	15.5
16.1.3	delaying the game (12 seconds shall be the maximum time from the end of a rally to the whistle for service under normal playing conditions);	
16.1.4	delaying the game by a team member.	

16.2 DELAY SANCTIONS

16.2.1	"*Delay warning*" and "*delay penalty*" are team sanctions.	
16.2.1.1	Delay sanctions remain in force for the entire match.	
16.2.1.2	All delay sanctions are recorded on the score sheet.	
16.2.2	The first delay in the match by a team member is sanctioned with a "DELAY WARNING".	D9 (25), D7b
16.2.3	The second and subsequent delays of any type by any member of the same team in the same match constitute a fault and are sanctioned with a "DELAY PENALTY": a point and service to the opponent.	D9 (25), D7b
16.2.4	Delay sanctions imposed before or between sets are applied in the following set.	

17 EXCEPTIONAL GAME INTERRUPTIONS

17.1 INJURY/ ILLNESS

17.1.1 Should a serious accident occur while the ball is in play, the referee must stop the game immediately and permit medical assistance to enter the court.

The rally is then replayed.

17.1.2 An injured/ill player is given a maximum of 5 minutes recovery time. The referee must authorize the properly accredited medical staff to enter the playing court to attend the player. Only the 1st referee may authorize a player to leave the playing area without penalty. When the treatment has been completed or if no treatment can be provided, play must resume. The 1st referee will whistle and request the player to continue. At this time, only the player can judge whether he/she is fit to play.

If the player does not recover or return to the playing area at the conclusion of the recovery time, his/her team is declared incomplete.   6.4.3, 7.3.1

In extreme cases, the doctor of the competition can oppose the return of an injured player.

Note: the recovery time will begin when the properly accredited medical staff member(s) of the competition arrives at the playing court to attend to the player. In the event that no accredited medical staff is available or in cases where the player chooses to be treated by his/her own medical personnel, the time will begin from the moment the recovery time was authorized by the referee.

17.2 EXTERNAL INTERFERENCE

If there is any external interference during the game, the play has to be stopped and the rally is replayed.

17.3 PROLONGED INTERRUPTIONS

17.3.1 If unforeseen circumstances interrupt the match, the 1st referee, the organizer and the Control Committee, if there is one, shall decide the measures to be taken to re-establish normal conditions.

17.3.2 Should one or several interruptions occur not exceeding 4 hours in total, the match is resumed with the score acquired, regardless of whether it continues on the same playing court or another playing court.

17.3.3 Should one or several interruptions occur, exceeding 4 hours in total, the whole match shall be replayed.

18 INTERVALS AND CHANGE OF COURTS/SWITCHES

18.1 INTERVALS

18.1.1 An interval is the time between sets. All intervals last one minute. D9 (3)

During this period of time, the change of courts (if requested) and service order of the teams on the score sheet are made.

During the interval before a deciding set, the referees carry out a toss in accordance with Rule 7.1.

18.2 COURT SWITCHES

18.2.1 The teams switch after every 7 points (Set 1 and 2) and 5 points (Set 3) played. D9 (3)

18.2.2 During court switches the teams must change immediately without delay.

If the court switch is not made at the proper time, it will take place as soon as the error is noticed.

The score at the time that the court switch is made remains the same.

CHAPTER 6
PARTICIPANTS' CONDUCT

See Rules

19 REQUIREMENTS OF CONDUCT

19.1 SPORTSMANLIKE CONDUCT

19.1.1 Participants must know the "Official Beach Volleyball Rules" and abide by them.

19.1.2 Participants must accept referees' decisions with sportsmanlike conduct, without disputing them.

In case of doubt, clarification may be requested only through the captain. 5.1.2.1

19.1.3 Participants must refrain from actions or attitudes aimed at influencing the decisions of the referees or covering up faults committed by their team.

19.2 FAIR PLAY

19.2.1 Participants must behave respectfully and courteously in the spirit of FAIR PLAY, not only towards the referees, but also towards other officials, the opponent, teammates and spectators.

19.2.2 Communication between team members during the match is permitted. 5.2.3.4

20 MISCONDUCT AND ITS SANCTIONS

20.1 MINOR MISCONDUCT

Minor misconduct offences are not subject to sanctions. It is the 1st referee's duty to prevent the teams from approaching the sanctioning level. 5.1.2, 21.3

This is done in two stages:

Stage 1: by issuing a verbal warning through the captain;

Stage 2: by use of a YELLOW CARD to a team member. This formal warning is not in itself a sanction but a symbol that the team member (and by extension the team) has reached the sanctioning level for the match. It is recorded in the score sheet but has no immediate consequences. D9 (5)

20.2 MISCONDUCT LEADING TO SANCTIONS

Incorrect conduct by a team member towards officials, opponents, teammates or spectators is classified in three categories according to the seriousness of the offence. — 4.1.1

20.2.1 Rude conduct: acting contrary to good manners or moral principles.

20.2.2 Offensive conduct: defamatory or insulting words or gestures including any action expressing contempt.

20.2.3 Aggression: actual physical attack or aggressive or threatening behaviour.

20.3 SANCTION SCALE

According to the judgment of the 1st referee and depending on the seriousness of the offence, the sanctions to be applied and recorded on the score sheet are: **Penalty, Expulsion or Disqualification.** — D7a

20.3.1 Penalty

For rude conduct or a single repetition of rude conduct in the same set by the same player. On each of the first two occasions, the team is sanctioned with a point and service to the opponents. A third rude conduct by a player in the same set is sanctioned by expulsion. Rude conduct sanctions may, however, be given to the same player in subsequent sets. — D9 (6)

20.3.2 Expulsion

The first offensive conduct is sanctioned by expulsion. The player who is sanctioned with expulsion must leave the playing area and his/her team is declared incomplete for the set. — 6.4.3, 7.3.1, D9 (7)

20.3.3 Disqualification

The first physical attack or implied or threatened aggression is sanctioned by disqualification. The player must leave the playing area and his/her team is declared incomplete for the match. — 6.4.3, 7.3.1, D9 (8)

MISCONDUCT is sanctioned as shown in the sanction scale. — D7a

20.4 MISCONDUCT BEFORE AND BETWEEN SETS

Any misconduct occurring before or between sets is sanctioned according to the sanction scale and the sanction is applied in the following set. — D7a

| 20.5 | SUMMARY OF MISCONDUCT AND CARDS USED | D9 (5, 6, 7, 8) |

Warning: no sanction – Stage 1: verbal warning　　　　　　20.1
　　　　　　　　　　Stage 2: symbol Yellow card

Penalty: sanction – symbol Red card　　　　　　　　　　　20.3.1, D7a

Expulsion: sanction – symbol Red + Yellow cards jointly　　20.3.2, D7a

Disqualification: sanction – symbol Red + Yellow card separately　20.3.3, D7a

附：本规则英文部分

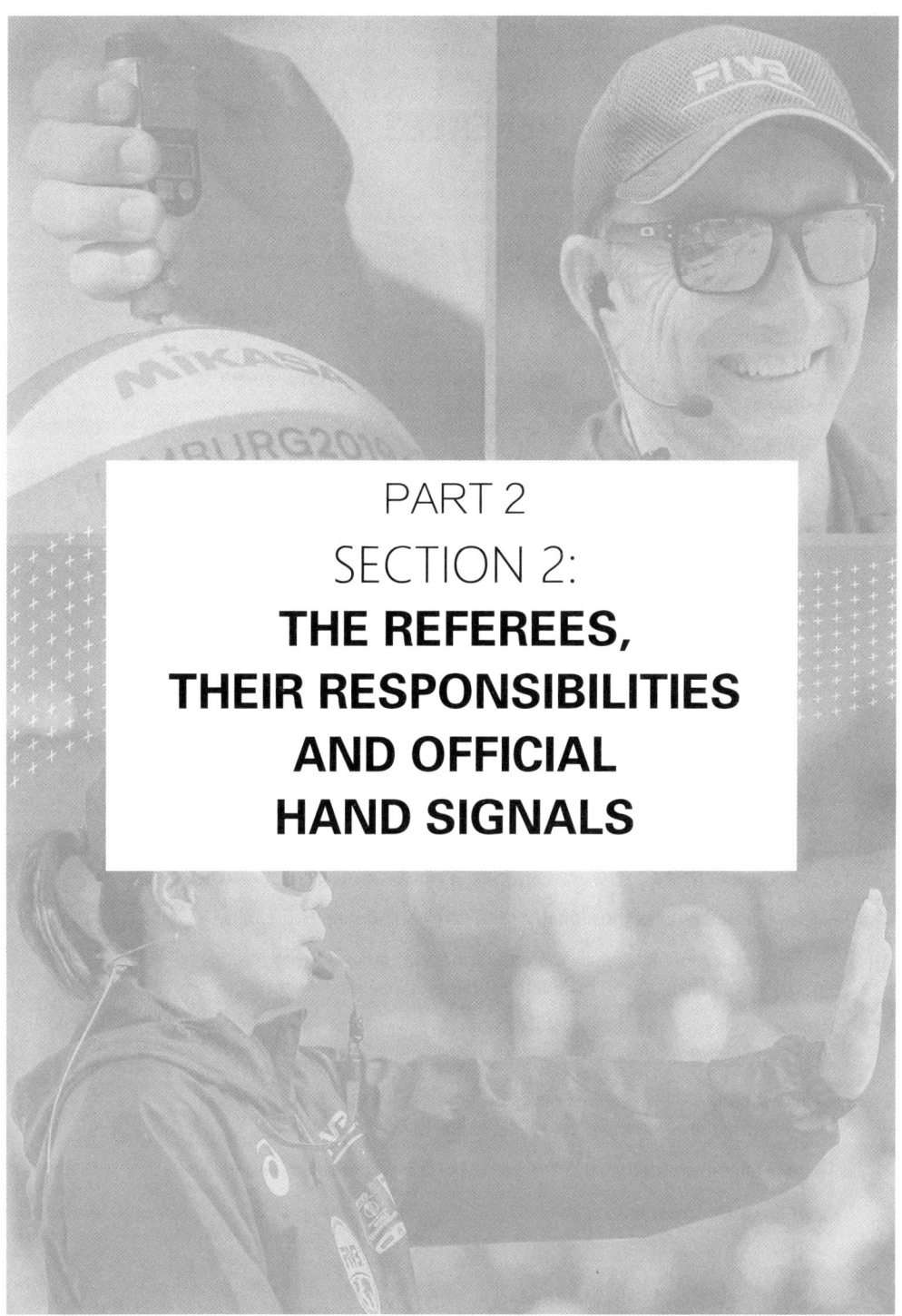

PART 2
SECTION 2:
THE REFEREES, THEIR RESPONSIBILITIES AND OFFICIAL HAND SIGNALS

CHAPTER 7
REFEREES

	See Rules

21 REFEREEING TEAM AND PROCEDURES

21.1 COMPOSITION

The refereeing team for a match is composed of the following officials:

	See Rules
– the 1st referee,	22
– the 2nd referee,	23
– the challenge referee (where applicable),	24
– the reserve referee (where applicable),	25
– the scorer,	26
– four (two) line judges.	28

Their location is shown in the Diagram 8.

For FIVB, World and Official Competitions, an assistant scorer is compulsory. — 27

21.2 PROCEDURES

		See Rules
21.2.1	Only the 1st and 2nd referees may blow a whistle during the match:	
21.2.1.1	the 1st referee gives the signal for the service that begins the rally.	D9 (1)
21.2.1.2	the 1st or 2nd referee signals the end of the rally, provided that they are sure that a fault has been committed and they have identified its nature.	
21.2.2	They may blow the whistle when the ball is out of play to indicate that they authorize or reject a team request.	
21.2.3	Immediately after the referee blows the whistle to signal **the completion** of the rally, they have to indicate with the official hand signals:	21.2.1.2, 29.1
21.2.3.1	If the fault is whistled by the 1st referee, he/she will indicate in order:	
	a) the team to serve,	D9 (2)
	b) the nature of the fault,	
	c) the player(s) at fault (if necessary).	

21.2.3.2 If the fault is whistled by the 2nd referee, he/she will indicate:

a) the nature of the fault,

b) the player at fault (if necessary),

c) the team to serve following the hand signal of the first referee. D9 (2)

In this case, the 1st referee does not show either the nature of the fault or the player at fault, but only the team to serve.

21.2.3.3 In the case of a double fault both referees indicate in order: D9 (23)

a) the nature of the fault,

b) the players at fault (if necessary),

The team to serve next is then indicated by the 1st referee. D9 (2)

22 1st REFEREE

22.1 LOCATION

The 1st referee carries out his/her functions standing on a referee's stand located at one end of the net on the opposite side to the scorer. His/her view must be approximately 50 cm above the net. D1, D8

22.2 AUTHORITY

22.2.1 The 1st referee directs the match from the start until the end. He/she has authority over all members of the refereeing team and the members of the teams.

During the match his/her decisions are final. He/she is authorized to overrule the decisions of other members of the refereeing team, if it is noticed that they are mistaken.

He/she may even replace a member of the refereeing team who is not performing his/her functions properly.

22.2.2 He/she also controls the work of the ball retrievers, and sand levellers.

22.2.3 He/she has the power to decide any matters involving the game, including those not provided for in the Rules.

22.2.4 He/she shall not permit any discussion about his/her decisions.

However, at the request of the captain, the 1st referee will give an explanation on the application or interpretation of the rules upon which he/she has based his/her decision.

If the captain disagrees with the explanation and formally protests, the 1st referee must authorize the commencement of a Protest Protocol.

22.2.5	The 1st referee is responsible for determining before and during the match whether the playing area and the conditions meet playing requirements.	
22.2.6	Depending on the circumstances leading up to an eventual injury/ illness of a player, the 1st referee authorizes the medical assistance and initiates the recovery time.	17.1.2

22.3 RESPONSIBILITIES

22.3.1 Prior to the match, the 1st referee:

22.3.1.1 inspects the conditions of the playing area, the balls and other equipment;

22.3.1.2 performs the toss with the team captains;

22.3.1.3 controls the teams' warming-up.

22.3.2 During the match, he/she is authorized:

22.3.2.1 to issue warnings to the teams;

22.3.2.2 to sanction misconduct and delays;

22.3.2.3 to decide upon:

a) the faults of the server and the screen of the serving team;	D5
b) the faults in playing the ball;	
c) the faults above the net, and the faulty contact of the player with the net, primarily (but not exclusively) on the attacker's side;	
d) the ball crossing completely the lower space under the net;	D9 (22)
e) the served ball and the 3rd hit passing over or outside the antenna on his/ her side of the court.	

22.3.3 At the end of the match, he/she checks the score sheet and signs it.

23 2nd REFEREE

23.1 LOCATION

The 2nd referee performs his/her functions standing outside the playing court near the post, on the opposite side of and facing the 1st referee.	D1, D8

23.2 AUTHORITY

23.2.1	The 2nd referee is the assistant of the 1st referee, but has also his/her own range of jurisdiction.	23.3
	Should the 1st referee be unable to continue his/her work, the 2nd	

	referee may replace him/her.	
23.2.2	He/she may, without whistling, also signal faults outside his/her range of jurisdiction, but must not insist upon them to the 1st referee.	
23.2.3	He/she controls the work of the scorer(s).	
23.2.4	He/she reports any misconduct to the 1st referee.	
23.2.5	He/she authorizes the time-outs and court switches, controls the duration of such and rejects improper requests.	D9 (3, 4)
23.2.6	He/she checks the number of time-outs used by each team and reports to the 1st referee and the players concerned after completion of their time-out.	
23.2.7	In the case the 1st referee authorizes medical assistance to a player, he/she assists in the process, including managing the recovery time.	17.1.2
23.2.8	He/she checks during the match that the balls still meet the requirements of the regulations.	
23.2.9	He/she conducts the toss between sets 2 and 3 if the 1st Referee is not able to do it. He/she then must pass all relevant information to the scorer.	

23.3 RESPONSIBILITIES

23.3.1	At the start of each set, and whenever necessary, the 2nd referee controls the work of the scorer and checks that the correct server has the ball.	
23.3.2	During the match, the 2nd referee decides, whistles and signals:	
23.3.2.1	interference due to penetration into the opponent's court and space under the net;	11.2, D9 (22)
23.3.2.2	the faulty contact of the player with the net primarily (but not exclusively) on the blocker's side and with the antenna on his/her side of the court;	11.3.1
23.3.2.3	the contact of the ball with an outside object;	8.4.2, 8.4.3 D9 (15), D10 (4)
23.3.2.4	the ball that crosses the net totally or partly outside the crossing space to the opponent court or touches the antenna on his/her side of the court, including during service;	8.4.3, 8.4.4, D3, D4a, D9 (15)
23.3.2.5	the contact of the ball with the sand when the 1st referee is not in position to see the contact;	
23.3.2.6	the ball recovered completely on the opponent's side under the net.	D9 (22)
23.3.2.7	the served ball and the 3rd hit passing over or outside the antenna on his/her side of the court.	

23.3.3 At the end of the match, he/she checks and signs the score sheet.

24 CHALLENGE REFEREE

For FIVB, World and Official Competitions if the Video Challenge System (VCS) is in use, a Challenge referee is compulsory.

24.1 LOCATION

The Challenge Referee carries out his/her functions in the challenge booth locating in a separate position determined by the FIVB Technical Delegate.

24.2 RESPONSIBILITIES

24.2.1 He/she supervises the challenge process and ensures, that it proceeds according to the challenge regulation in force.

24.2.2 The Challenge referee shall wear an official referee uniform while performing his/her functions.

24.2.3 After the challenge process he/she advises the 1st referee of the nature of the fault.   21.2.3.1, D9 (2)

24.2.4 At the end of the match, he/she signs the score sheet.

25 RESERVE REFEREE

For FIVB, World and Official Competitions a Reserve referee is compulsory for all TV matches, and anytime the Video Challenge System (VCS) is in use.

25.1 LOCATION

The Reserve referee carries out his/her functions locating in a separate position determined by the FIVB court layout.

25.2 RESPONSIBILITIES

The Reserve referee is obliged to:

25.2.1 Wear an official referee uniform while performing his/her functions.

25.2.2 Replace the 2nd referee in case of absence or in case that he/she is unable to continue his/her work or in case that the 2nd referee became the 1st referee.   23.2.1

25.2.3 Assist the 2nd referee in keeping the free zone.   D9

25.2.4 Bring to the 2nd referee four match balls, immediately after the presentation of the players.   3.3

25.2.5	Give the 2nd referee a match ball after he/she has finished checking the player at service.	22.2.2
25.2.6	Assist the 1st referee with guiding the work of the sand levellers.	
25.2.7	In case the Video Challenge System (VCS) is in use, he/she supervises the Scorer in filling in the Challenge System process at the e-score sheet.	24

26 SCORER

26.1 LOCATION

The scorer performs his/her functions seated at the scorer's table on the opposite side of the court from and facing the 1st referee.	D1, D8

26.2 RESPONSIBILITIES

The scorer fills in the score sheet according to the Rules, cooperating with the 2nd referee.

He/she uses a buzzer or other sound device to notify irregularities or give signals to the referees on the basis of his/her responsibilities.

26.2.1   Prior to the match and set, the scorer:

26.2.1.1 registers the data of the match and teams, according to procedures in force and obtains the signatures of the captains;

26.2.1.2 records the service order of each team.

26.2.2   During the match, the scorer:

26.2.2.1 records the points scored;

26.2.2.2 controls the serving order of each team and indicates any error before the service hit;

26.2.2.3 records the time-outs, checking the number of such, and informs the 2nd referee;

26.2.2.4	notifies the referees of a request for time-out that is improper;	15.5

26.2.2.5 announces to the referees the court switches and the end of the sets;

26.2.2.6 records any sanctions and improper requests;

26.2.2.7 records all other events as instructed by the 2nd referee, i.e. recovery time, prolonged interruptions, external interference, etc.;

26.2.2.8 controls the interval between sets:

26.2.3   At the end of the match, the scorer;

26.2.3.1 records the final result;

26.2.3.2 in the case of a protest, with the previous authorization of the 1st referee, writes or permits the captain concerned to write on the score sheet a statement on the incident being protested;   5.1.2.1, 5.1.3.2

26.2.3.3 signs the score sheet, before he/she obtains the signatures of the team captains and then the referees.

27 ASSISTANT SCORER

27.1 LOCATION

The assistant scorer performs his/her functions seated beside the scorer at the scorer's table.   D1, D8

27.2 RESPONSIBILITIES

He/she assists with the administrative duties of the scorer's work.

Should the scorer become unable to continue his/her work, the assistant scorer substitutes for the scorer.

27.2.1 Prior to the match and set, the assistant scorer:

27.2.1.1 checks that all information displayed at the scoreboard(s) is correct,

27.2.2 During the match, the assistant scorer:

27.2.2.1 indicates the serving order of each team by displaying a sign numbered 1 or 2 corresponding to the player to serve and,

27.2.2.2 indicates by use of the buzzer any error to the referees immediately;

27.2.2.3 operates the manual scoreboard on the scorer's table;

27.2.2.4 checks that the scoreboards agree;

27.2.2.5 starts and ends the timing of the Technical Time-outs;

27.2.2.6 if necessary, updates the reserve score sheet and gives it to the scorer;

27.2.3 At the end of the match, the assistant scorer:

27.2.3.1 signs the score sheet.

28 LINE JUDGES

28.1 LOCATION

If only two line judges are used, they stand at the corners of the court closest to the right hand of each referee, diagonally at 1 to 2m from the corner.   D1, D8

Each one of them controls both the end line and side line on his/her side.

For FIVB, World and Official Competitions, if four line judges are used, they stand in the free zone at 1 to 3 m from each corner of the court, on the imaginary extension of the line that they control.

28.2 RESPONSIBILITIES

28.2.1	The line judges perform their functions by using flags (40 x 40 cm), to signal:	D10
28.2.1.1	the ball "in" and "out" whenever the ball lands near their line(s) (Note: it is primarily the line judge closest to the path of the ball who is responsible for the signal);	8.3, 8.4 D10 (1, 2)
28.2.1.2	the touches of "out" balls by the team receiving the ball;	8.4, D10 (3)
28.2.1.3	the ball touching the antenna, the served ball and the third hit of the team crossing the net outside the crossing space, etc.;	8.4.3, 8.4.4, 10.1.1, D4a, D10 (4)
28.2.1.4	any player (except the server) stepping outside of his/her court at the moment of the service hit;	7.4, 12.4.3, D10 (4)
28.2.1.5	the foot faults of the server;	12.4.3, D10 (4)
28.2.1.6	any contact with the top 80 cm of the antenna on their side of the court by any player during his/her action of playing the ball or interfering with the play;	11.3.1, 11.4.4, D3, D10 (4)
28.2.1.7	the ball crossing the net outside the crossing space into the opponent's court or touching the antenna on his/her side of the court.	10.1.1, D4a, D10 (4)
28.2.1.8	the block touches during the rally.	
28.2.2	At the first referee's request, a line judge must repeat his/her signal.	

29 OFFICIAL SIGNALS

29.1 REFEREES' HAND SIGNALS

The referees will indicate with the official hand signal the reason for their whistle (the nature of the fault whistled or the purpose of the interruption authorized). The signal has to be maintained for a moment and, if it is indicated with one hand, the hand corresponds to the side of the team which has made the fault or the request.   D9

29.2 LINE JUDGES' FLAG SIGNALS

The line judges must indicate with the official flag signal the nature of the fault called, and maintain the signal for a moment.   D10

附：本规则英文部分

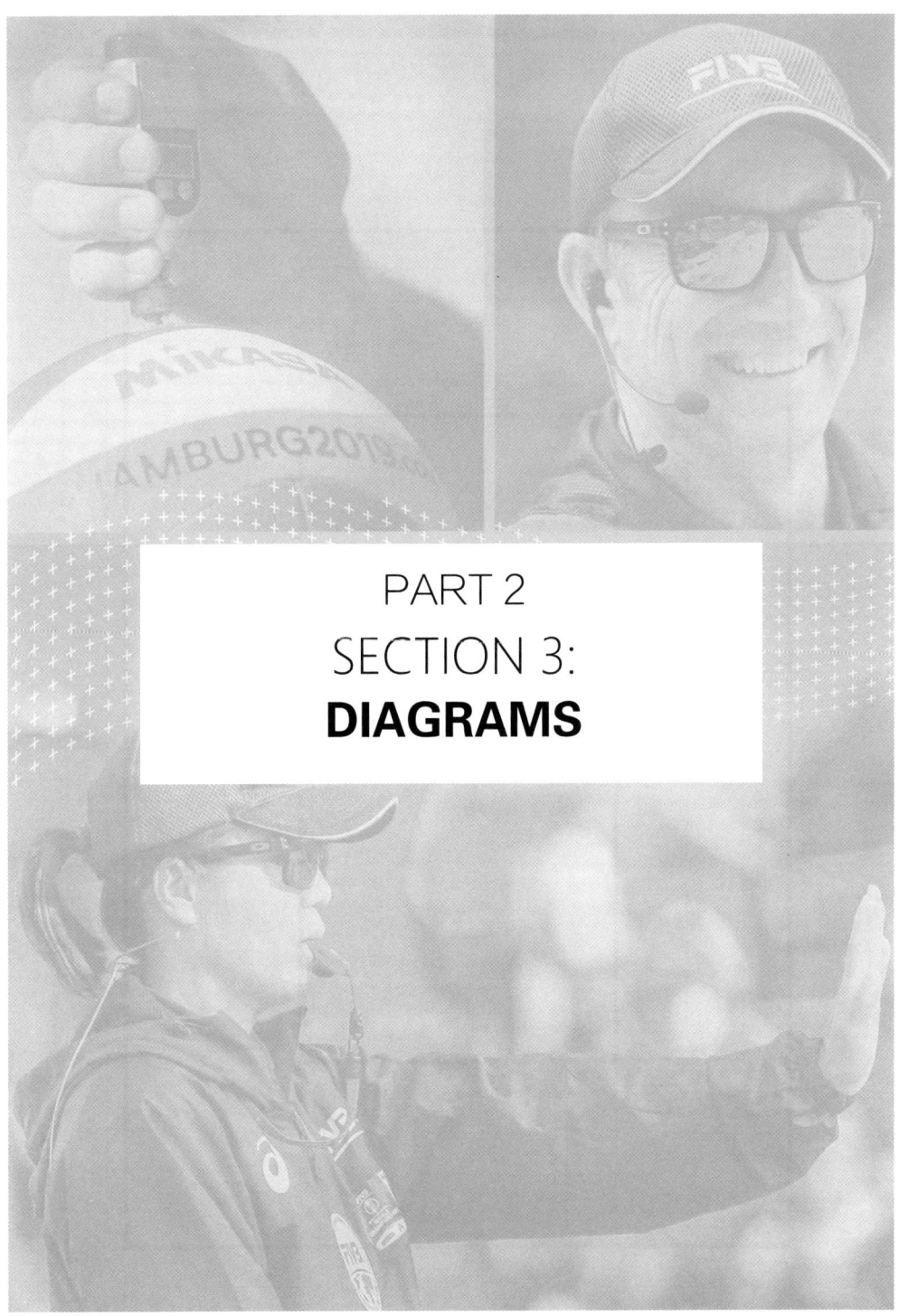

PART 2
SECTION 3:
DIAGRAMS

DIAGRAM 1: THE PLAYING AREA

Relevant Rules: 1, 22.1, 23.1, 26.1, 27.1, 28.1

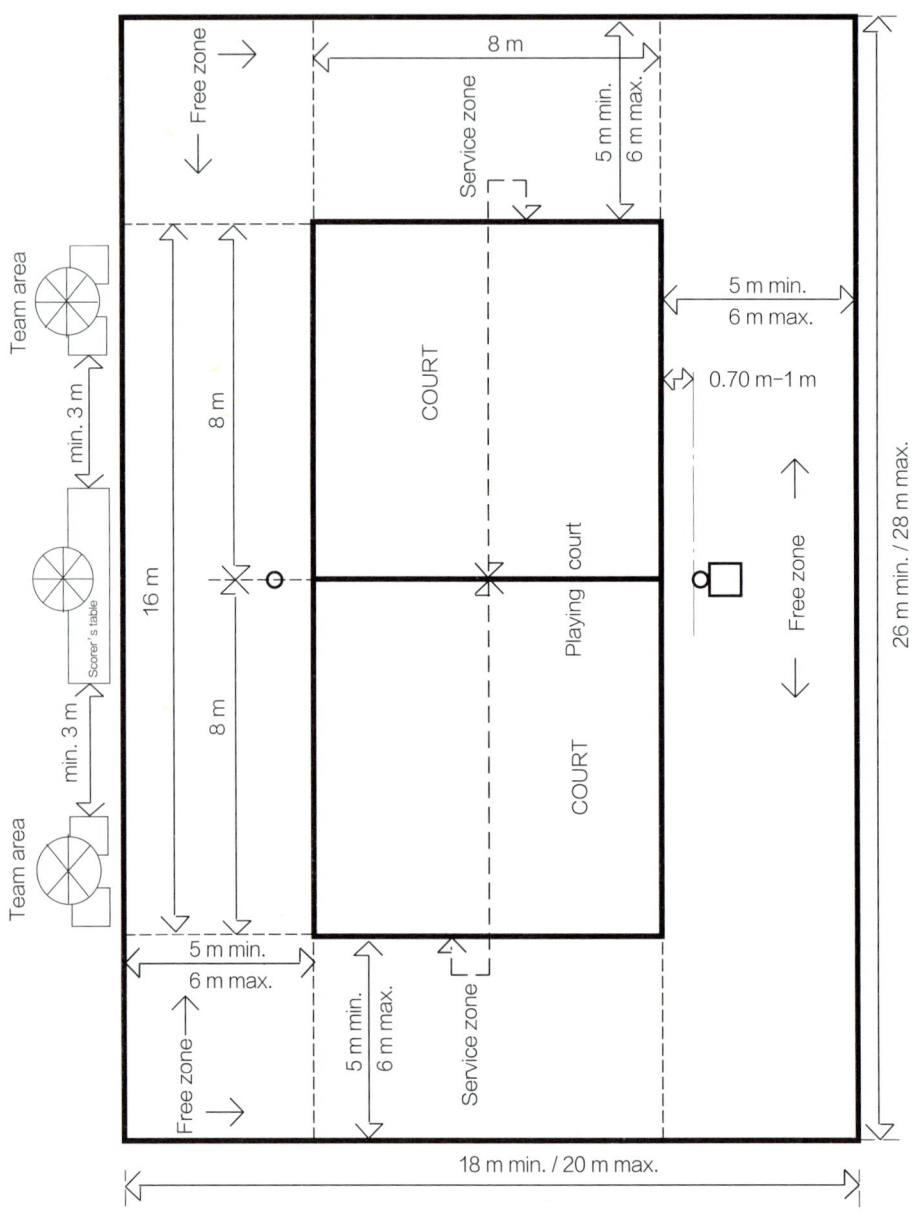

DIAGRAM 2: THE PLAYING COURT

Relevant Rules: 1.1, 1.3, 2.5

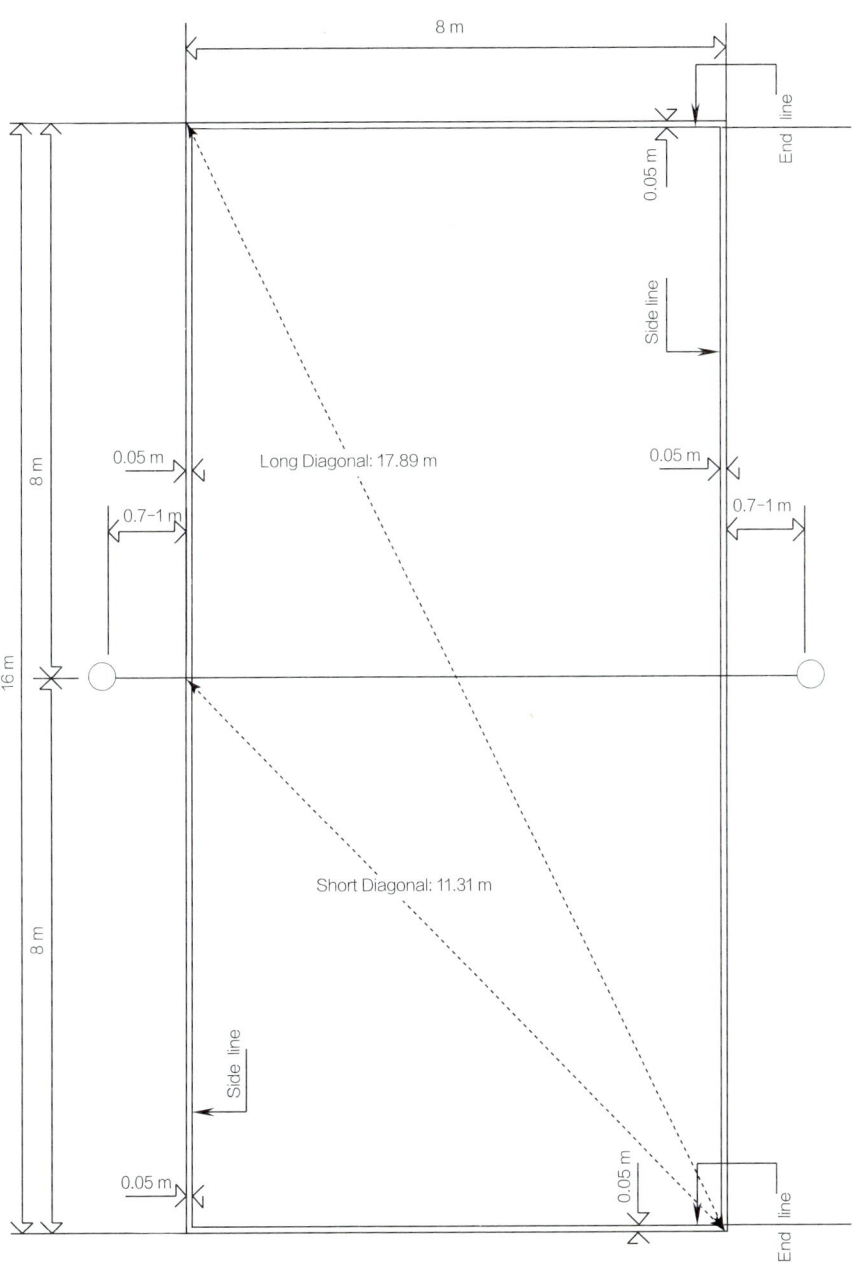

DIAGRAM 3: DESIGN OF THE NET

Relevant Rules: 2, 8.4.3

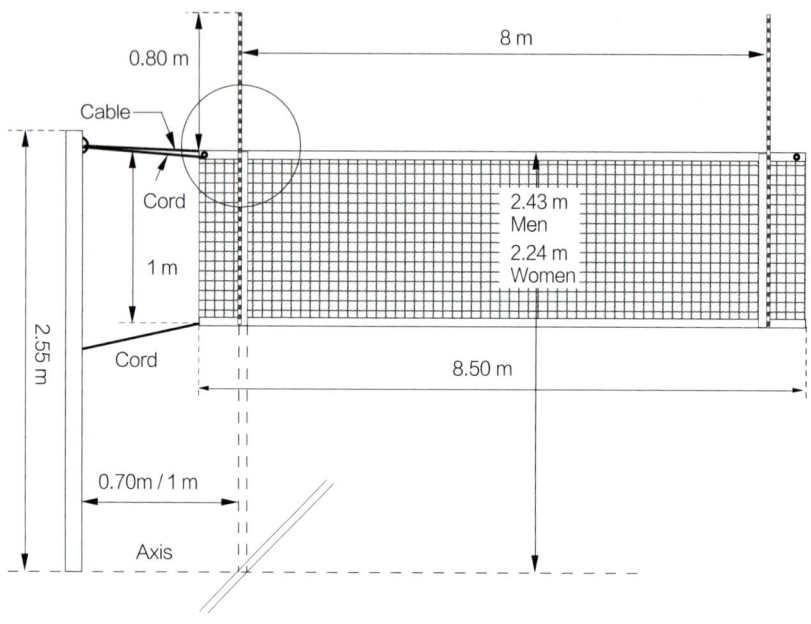

For FIVB, World and Official Competitions, the net may be adjusted according 2.1 above.

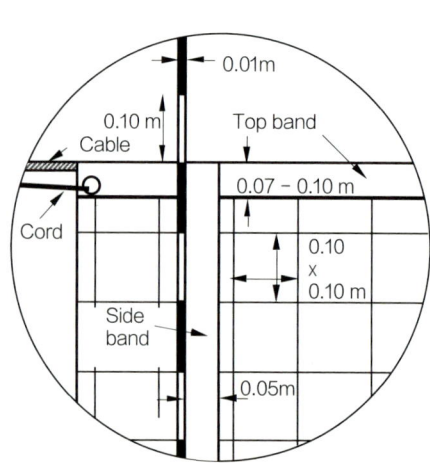

DIAGRAM 4a: BALL CROSSING THE VERTICAL PLANE OF THE NET TO THE OPPONENT COURT

Relevant Rules: 8.4.3, 8.4.4, 8.4.5, 10.1.1, 23.3.2.4, 28.2.1.3, 28.2.1.7

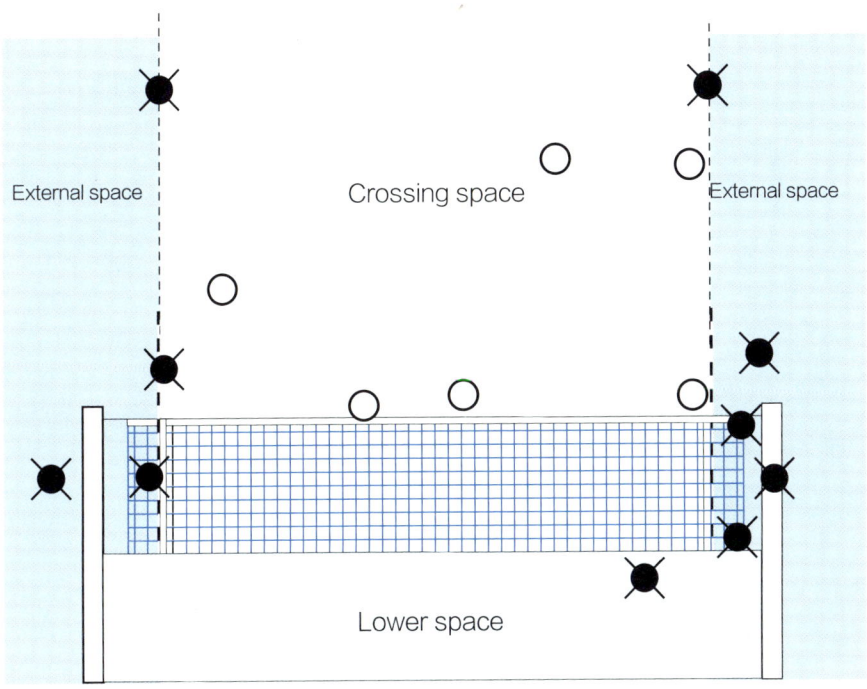

DIAGRAM 4b: BALL CROSSING THE VERTICAL PLANE OF THE NET TO THE OPPONENT FREE ZONE

Relevant Rules: 10.1.2, 10.1.2.1

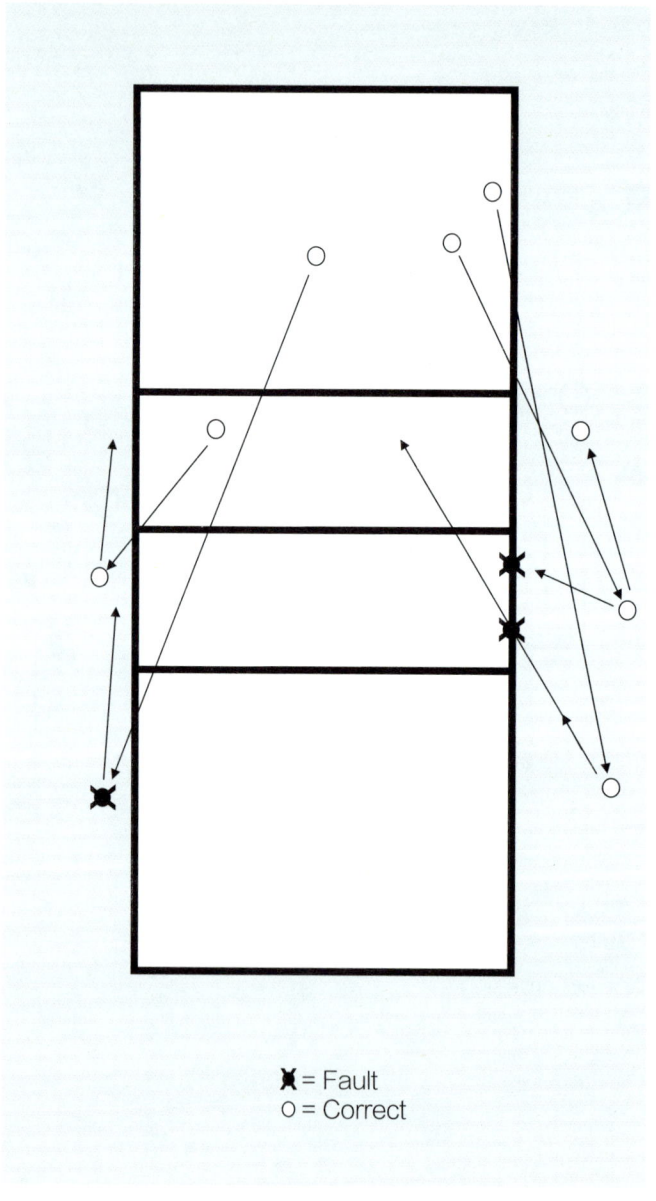

DIAGRAM 5: SCREEN

Relevant Rules: 12.5.1, 12.5.2, 12.6.2.3, 22.3.2.3

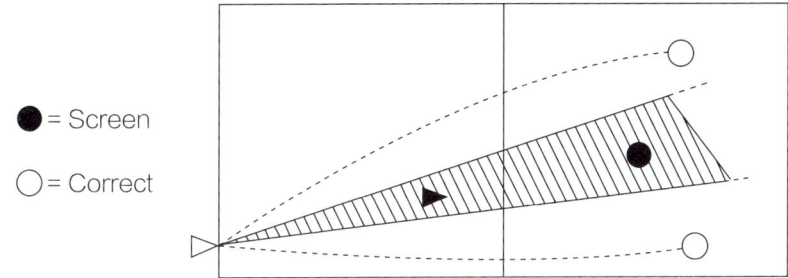

● = Screen
○ = Correct

DIAGRAM 6: COMPLETED BLOCK

Relevant Rule: 14.1.3

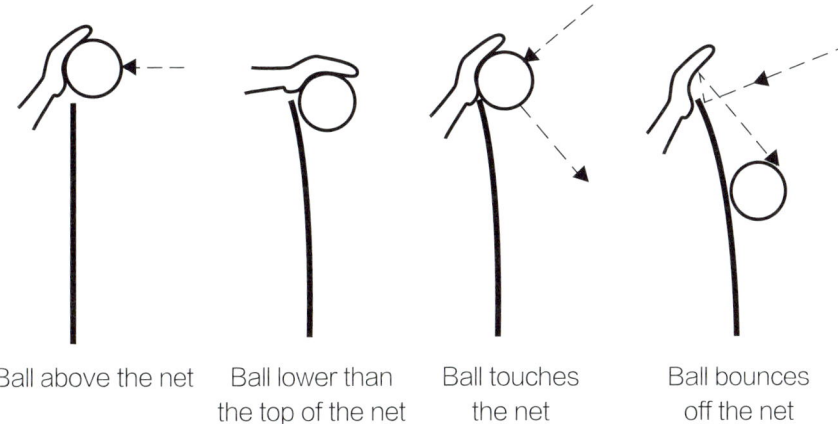

Ball above the net   Ball lower than the top of the net   Ball touches the net   Ball bounces off the net

DIAGRAM 7: DETERRENTS AND SANCTIONS

7a: MISCONDUCT WARNING AND SANCTIONS SCALE AND THEIR CONSEQUENCES

Relevant Rules: 20.3, 20.4, 20.5

CATEGORIES	OCCURRENCE	OFFENDER	SANCTION	CARDS	CONSEQUENCE
MINOR MISCONDUCT	Stage 1	Any member	Not considered as sanction	None	Prevention only
	Stage 2			Yellow	
	repetition any time		Considered as rude conduct	as below	as below
RUDE CONDUCT (same set)	First	Any member	Penalty	Red	A point and service to the opponent
	Second	Same member	Penalty	Red	A point and service to the opponent
	Third	Same member	Expulsion	Red + Yellow jointly	Team declared incomplete for the set
RUDE CONDUCT (new set)	First	Any member	Penalty	Red	A point and service to the opponent
OFFENSIVE CONDUCT	First	Any member	Expulsion	Red + Yellow jointly	Team declared incomplete for the set
	Second	Same member	Disqualification	Red + Yellow separately	Team declared incomplete for the match
AGGRESSION	First	Any member	Disqualification	Red + Yellow separately	Team declared incomplete for the match

7b: DELAY SANCTIONS SCALE AND CONSEQUENCES

Relevant Rules: 16.2.2, 16.2.3

CATEGORIES	OCCURRENCE	OFFENDER	DETERRENT or SANCTION	CARDS	CONSEQUENCE
DELAY	First	Any member of the team	Delay Warning	Hand signal No. 25 with Yellow card	Prevention–no penalty
	Second and subsequent	Any member of the team	Delay Penalty	Hand signal No. 25 with Red card	A point and service to the opponent

DIAGRAM 8: LOCATION OF REFEREEING TEAM AND THEIR ASSISTANTS

Relevant Rules: 3.3, 21.1, 22.1, 23.1, 26.1, 27.1, 28.1

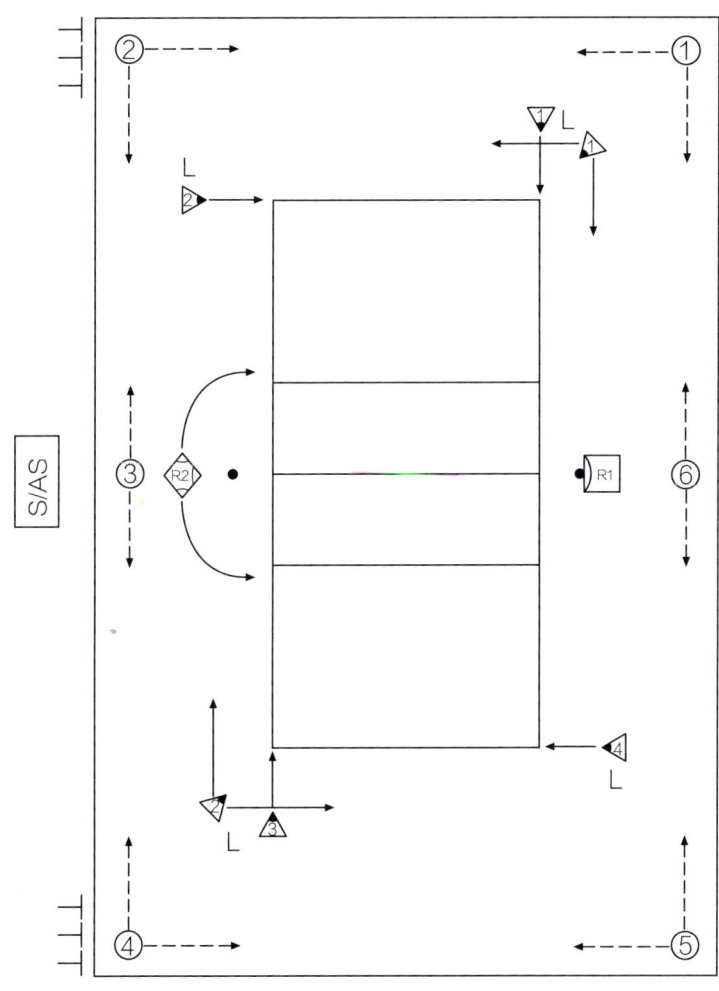

[R1] = First Referee
[R2] = Second Referee
S/AS = Scorer/Assistant Scorer
▷ = Lines Judges (numbers 1-4 or 1-2)
④ = Ball Retrievers (numbers 1-6)
⊣ = Sand Levelers

DIAGRAM 9: REFEREES' OFFICIAL HAND SIGNALS

Legend: Ⓕ Ⓢ Referee(s) who must show the signal according to their regular responsibilities
　　　　 Ⓕ Ⓢ Referee(s) who show the signal in special situations

1 AUTHORISATION TO SERVE

Relevant Rules: 12.3, 21.2.1.1

Move the hand to indicate direction of service

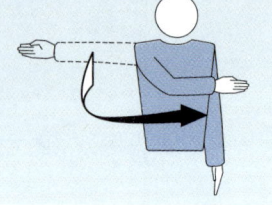

2 TEAM TO SERVE

Relevant Rules: 12.3, 21.2.3.1a, 21.2.3.2c, 21.2.3.3c

Extend the arm to the side of team that will serve

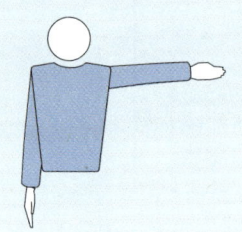

3 CHANGE OF COURTS

Relevant Rules: 18.2, 23.2.5

Raise the forearms front and back and twist them around the body

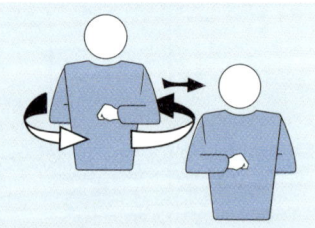

4 TIME-OUT

Relevant Rules: 15, 23.2.5

Place the palm of one hand over the fingers of the other, held vertically (forming a T) and then indicate the requesting team

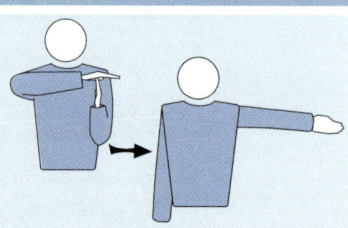

附：本规则英文部分

5　MISCONDUCT WARNING

Relevant Rules: 20.1, 20.5

Show a yellow card for warning

🅕

6　MISCONDUCT PENALTY

Relevant Rules: 20.3.1, 20.5

Show a red card for penalty

7　EXPULSION

Relevant Rules: 20.3.2, 20.5

Show both cards jointly for expulsion

8　DISQUALIFICATION

Relevant Rules: 20.3.3, 20.5

Show red and yellow cards separately for disqualification

9	END OF SET (OR MATCH)

Relevant Rules: 6.2, 6.3

Cross the forearms in front of the chest, hands open

10	BALL NOT TOSSED OR RELEASED AT THE SERVICE HIT

Relevant Rule: 12.4.1

Lift the extended arm, the palm of the hand facing upwards

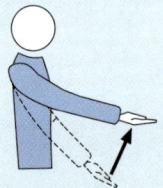

11	DELAY IN SERVICE

Relevant Rule: 12.4.4

Raise five fingers, spread open

12	BLOCKING FAULT OR SCREENING

Relevant Rules: 12.5, 14.5, 14.6.3

Raise both arms vertically, palms forward

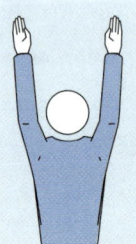

13   POSITIONAL OR ROTATIONAL FAULT

Relevant Rules: 7.7.1, 12.6.1.1

Make a circular motion with the forefinger

14   BALL "IN"

Relevant Rules: 6.1.1.1, 8.3

Point the arm and fingers toward the floor

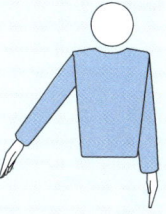

15   BALL "OUT"

Relevant Rules: 8.4.1, 8.4.2, 8.4.3, 8.4.4, 12.6.2.2, 13.2.2

Raise the forearms vertically, hands open,
palms towards the body

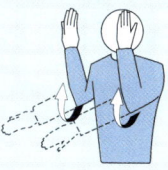

16   CATCH

Relevant Rules: 6.1.2, 9.3.3, 22.3.2.3b

Slowly lift the forearm, palm of the hand facing upwards

17	DOUBLE CONTACT

Relevant Rules: 6.1.2, 9.1.1, 9.3.4, 22.3.2.3b

Raise two fingers, spread open

18	FOUR HITS

Relevant Rule: 9.3.1

Raise four fingers, spread open

19	NET TOUCHED BY PLAYER – SERVED BALL TOUCHES THE NET BETWEEN THE ANTENNAE AND DOES NOT PASS THE VERTICAL PLANE OF THE NET

Relevant Rule: 12.6.2.1

Indicate the relevant side of the net with the corresponding hand

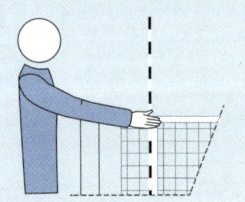

20	REACHING BEYOND THE NET

Relevant Rules: 11.4.1, 13.2.1

Place a hand above the net, palm facing downwards

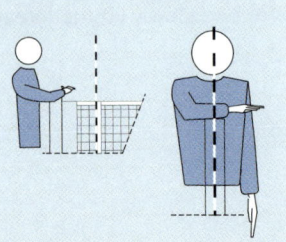

附：本规则英文部分

21   ATTACK HIT FAULT

– by a player who completes an attack-hit using an open-handed finger action, or if using finger tips that are not rigid and together.
– by a player who completes an attack hit on the opponent's service, when the ball is entirely higher than the top of the net.
– by a player who completes an attack-hit using an overhand pass which has a trajectory not perpendicular to the line of the shoulders, except when he/she is attempting to set to his or her teammate.

Relevant Rules: 13.2.3, 13.2.4, 13.2.5

Make a downward motion with the forearm, hand open

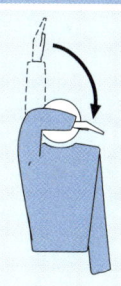

22   INTERFERENCE DUE TO PENETRATION INTO THE OPPONENT'S COURT AND SPACE UNDER THE NET
BALL CROSSES COMPLETELY THE LOWER SPACE UNDER THE NET
THE SERVER TOUCHES THE COURT (THE END LINE INCLUDED) OR THE GROUND OUTSIDE THE SERVICE ZONE
UNLESS FOR THE SERVER, THE PLAYER STEPS OUTSIDE HIS/HER COURT AT THE MOMENT OF THE SERVICE HIT

Relevant Rules: 8.4.5, 11.2.1, 12.4.3, 23.3.2.1, 23.3.2.6

Point to the court under the net or to the respective line

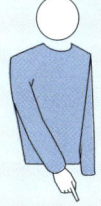

23   DOUBLE FAULT AND REPLAY

Relevant Rules: 6.1.2.2, 12.4.5

Raise both thumbs vertically

24   BALL TOUCHED

Relevant Rule: 14.6.4

Brush with the palm of one hand the fingers of the other, held vertically

25 DELAY WARNING / DELAY PENALTY

Relevant Rules: 15.5.5, 16.2.2, 16.2.3

Cover the wrist with a yellow card (warning) or with a red card (penalty)

附：本规则英文部分

DIAGRAM 10: LINE JUDGES' OFFICIAL FLAG SIGNALS

1   BALL "IN"

Relevant Rules: 8.3, 28.2.1.1

Point down with flag

2   BALL "OUT"

Relevant Rules: 8.4.1, 28.2.1.1

Raise flag vertically

3   BALL TOUCHED

Relevant Rule: 28.2.1.2

Raise flag and touch the top with the palm of the free hand

4   CROSSING SPACE FAULTS, BALL TOUCHED AN OUTSIDE OBJECT, OR FOOT FAULT BY ANY PLAYER DURING SERVICE

Relevant Rules: 8.4.2, 8.4.3, 8.4.4, 12.4.3, 28.2.1.3, 28.2.1.4, 28.2.1.5, 28.2.1.6, 28.2.1.7

Wave flag over the head and point to the antenna or the respective line

5 JUDGEMENT IMPOSSIBLE

Raise and cross both arms and hands in front of the chest

L

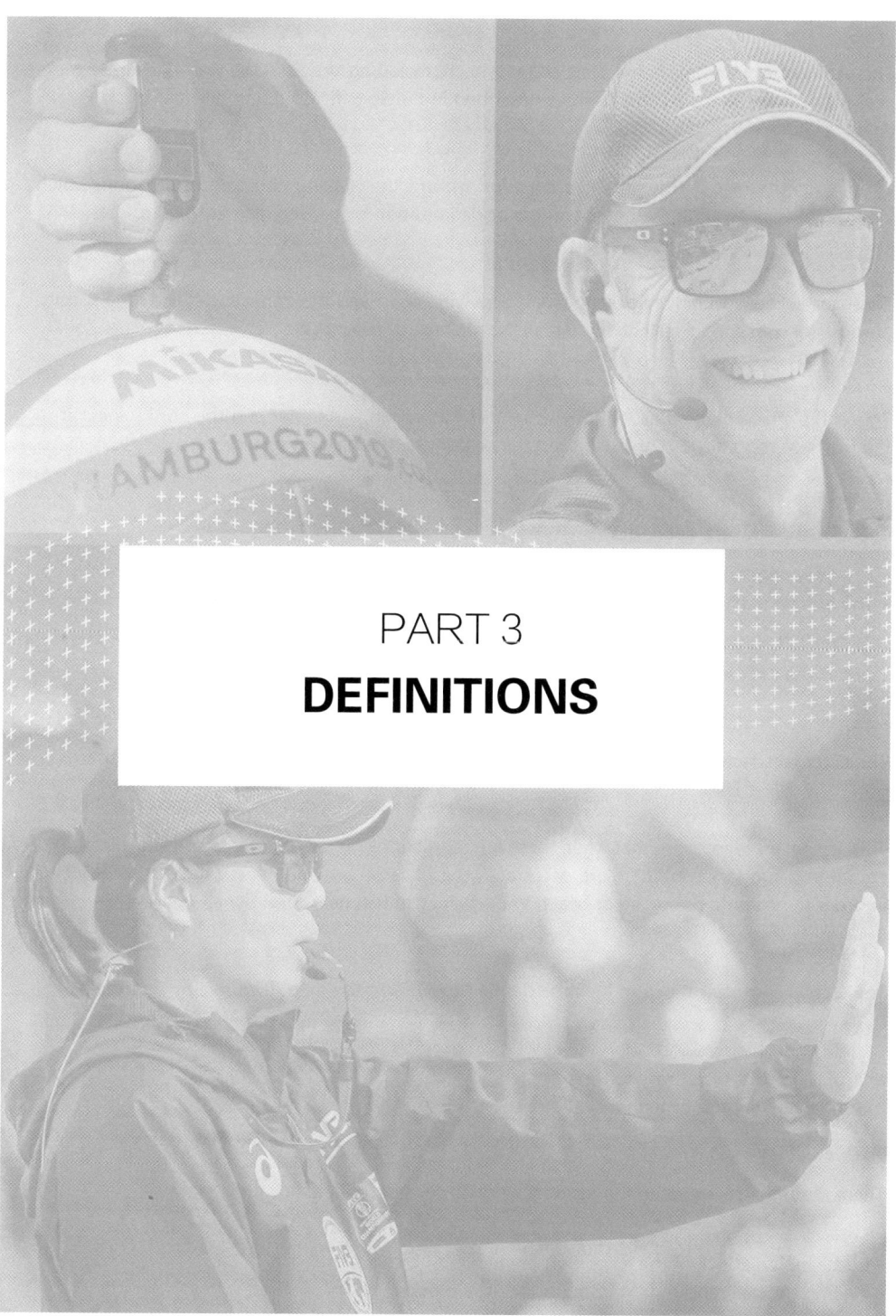

PART 3
DEFINITIONS

PROTOCOL

The series of events before the start of the match, including the toss, the warming-up session, presentation of the teams and referees described in the Specific Competition Handbook.

COMPETITION/ CONTROL AREA

The Competition/ Control Area is a corridor around the playing court and free zone, which includes all spaces up to the outer barriers or delimitation fence. See diagram/fig 1a.

ZONES

These are sections within the playing area (i.e. playing court and free zone) as defined for a specific purpose (or with special restrictions) within the rule text. These include: Service Zone & Free Zone.

LOWER SPACE

This is the space defined as its upper part by the bottom of the net and the cord joining it to the posts, at the sides by the posts, and the bottom by the playing surface.

CROSSING SPACE

The crossing space is defined by:

– The horizontal band at the top of the net
– The antennae and their extension
– The ceiling

The ball must cross to the opponent's COURT through the crossing space.

EXTERNAL SPACE

The external space is in the vertical plane of the net outside of the crossing and lower spaces.

UNLESS BY AGREEMENT OF FIVB

This statement recognizes that while there are regulations on the standards and specification of equipment and facilities, there are occasions when special arrangements can be made by FIVB in order to promote the game of Beach Volleyball or to test new conditions.

FIVB STANDARDS

The technical specifications or limits as defined by FIVB to the manufacturers of equipment.

FAULT

a) A playing action contrary to the rules.
b) A rule violation other than a playing action.

FIRST HIT OF THE TEAM

There are three cases, when the playing action is considered first hit of the team:

– Service reception
– Receiving an attack of the opponent team
– Playing the ball rebounding from opponent's block

RALLY POINT

This is the system of scoring a point whenever a rally is won.

TECHNICAL TIME-OUT

This special mandatory time-out is, in addition to time-outs, to allow the promotion of Beach Volleyball, analysis of the play and to allow additional commercial opportunities. Technical Time-Outs are mandatory for FIVB, World and Official competitions.

INTERVAL

The time between sets. The change of courts in the third (deciding) set is not to be regarded as an interval.

INTERFERING

Any action which will create an advantage against the opponent team or any action which prevents an opponent from playing the ball.

OUTSIDE OBJECT

An object or a person which while outside the playing court or close to the limit of the free playing space provides an obstruction to the flight of the ball. For example: Overhead lights, the referee's chair, TV equipment, scorer's table, and net posts. Outside objects do not include the antennae since they are considered as the part of the net.

BALL RETRIEVERS

These are personnel whose job it is to maintain the flow of the game by rolling the ball to the server between rallies.

SAND LEVELLERS (RAKERS)

These court assistants use long rakes or long poles with flattened ends to smooth out the sand especially around the court lines and across the central axis of the court between the posts.

INDEX

A
Additional Equipment 15
Antennae 14
Attack hit 28
Authorization of the service 27

B
Ball at the net 24
Ball crossing the net 24
Ball "in" 22, 59, 63
Ball in play 22
Ball in the net 25
Ball "out" 22, 59, 63
Ball out of play 22
Ball touching the net 25
Balls 15
Block 28, 53
Block and team hits 29
Block contact 29
Blocking 28, 58
Blocking faults 29
Blocking the service 29
Blocking within the opponent's space 29

C
Captain 17
Challenge Referee 42
– Location 42
– Responsibilities 42
Change of courts/switches 33, 56
Change of equipment 17
Characteristics of the attack hit 28
Characteristics of the hit 23
Contact with the net 25

D
Default and incomplete team 20
Delay sanctions 31
Dimensions 12

E
Equipment 16
Exceptional game interruption 32
Execution of the service 27
External interference 32

F
Fair play 34
Faults in playing the ball 24
Faults made during the service 27
Faults of the attack hit 28
First Referee 39
– Authority 39
– Location 39
– Responsibilities 40
First service in a set 26
Forbidden objects 17
Four-ball system 15

G
Game delays 31
Game interruptions 30

H
Height of the net 13

I
Improper request 31
Injury/ Illness 32
Interruptions 30
Intervals 33
Intervals and court switches 33

L
Lighting 13
Line judges 44, 63-64
– Location 44
– Responsibilities 45
Line judges' flag signals 45, 63-64
Lines on the court 13
Location of the team 16

M
Minor misconduct 34
Misconduct and its sanctions 34
Misconduct before and between sets 35
Misconduct leading to sanctions 35

N
Net and posts 13
Number of regular game interruptions . . . 30

O
Official signals 45, 56-62, 63-64
Official warm-up session 21

P
Player's faults at the net 26
Playing area 12, 48
Playing surface 12
Playing the ball 22
Positions 21
Positional fault 21
Posts 15
Prolonged interruptions 32

R
Reaching beyond the net 25, 60
Refereeing team 38, 55
– Procedures 38
– Responsibilities 40, 41, 42, 43, 44, 45
Referees' hand signals 45, 56-62
Requirements of conduct 34
Reserve Referee 42
– Location 42
– Responsibilities 42
Rotational fault 59

S
Sanction cards 36, 54, 57
Sanction scale 35, 54
Scorer 43
– Location 43
– Responsibilities 43
Screening 27, 58
Second Referee 40
– Authority 40
– Location 40
– Responsibilities 41
Service 26
Sequence of regular game interruptions ... 30
Service order 21
Service order faults 27
Side bands 14
Sportsmanlike conduct 34
Standards 15
States of play 22
Structure 14
Structure of play 20

T
Teams 16
Team composition 16
Team hits 23, 29
Team leaders 17
Team line-up 21
The toss 20
Time-out and Technical Time-out 30
To score a point 19
To score a point, win a set and the match .. 19
To win a set 20
To win the match 20
Types of delays 31

U
Uniformity of balls 15

V
Video Challenge System 42

W
Weather 13

Z
Zones and areas 13

MEMO

fivb.com